Globish

The World Over

By Jean Paul Nerrière and David Hon

A book written IN Globish

Globish The World Over

US Copyright Registry Case #1-206193066

ISBN 978-0-578-02879-8

International
globish
Institute

Table of Contents

Beginning

What if 50% of the world badly needed a certain communication tool, but only 5% could have it?

Someone would find a way. For example, to solve the problem of talking, they gave us handsets for little money and charge us by the minute. But that only does part of it. What will we *say* to each other?

The English language seems to be the most important communication tool for the international world. But now it must be a kind of English which can be learned quickly and used very easily – not like Standard English. The people who know a little are already using what they know. It works for them – a little. But… they often have families and jobs. They cannot spend enough time or enough money to learn all of English. And English speakers think these people will "never be good enough" in English. It is a problem. We think Globish is a solution.

Globish has a different name because it is a very different way to solve the problem of learning English. Using the standards of the Council of Europe Framework of Reference for Languages (page 64):

Globish speakers will use an amount of English that makes understanding between non-native speakers and native speakers. They will produce clear, detailed writing on a wide range of subjects and explain their thoughts, giving good and bad elements of various ideas.

This book is *about* Globish and to demonstrate its value, we'll write this book for you *in Globish*.

Part 1

The Problem

with Learning English

Chapter 1
Many, Many Languages

A hundred years ago, most human beings could speak two or more languages. At home they spoke a family language. It could be the language their parents spoke when they moved from another place. In many cases, it was a local variation of a language with different words and different pronunciations, what some people might call a dialect or patois. Most villages had such languages. People learned family languages, village languages and sometimes other languages without any problems.

A century ago, for most people the world was not very big, perhaps as big as their nation. They learned their national language and then could communicate with the rest of their world. Many nations had at least one official national language. Many people in their villages also felt a need to speak the national language, and they would learn that national language in schools.

National languages made nation-wide communication possible. In some cases these started as one of the local dialects and were raised to the status of national languages. Or sometimes one "family" was more powerful, and required everyone to speak their way.

Today, the communication problem is the same. Just the scale is different. A century ago, their world was their country. Now their world is.... much more. Most people now speak a local language which is often their national language. Now they must communicate to the whole globe.

(From English Next)

In this world, teachers say there are more than 6000 languages. In 45 countries, English is an official

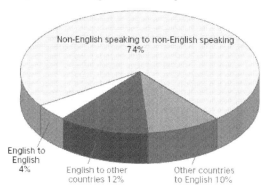

language. But not everyone speaks English, even where it is an official language. Only 12% of the global world has English as a mother tongue. For 88% of us, it is not our first language, our mother tongue.

We know that only 4% of international communication is between native speakers from different English-speaking nations - like Americans and Australians. So 96% of the international English communication takes place with at least one non-native speaker.

There is a story about a god and a Tower of Babel, where all men could speak to each other using just one language. In the story, he stopped the building of that special Tower. He said (roughly):

> *"Look, they are one people, and they have all one language. This is only the beginning of what they will do. Nothing that they want to do will be impossible now. Come, let us go down and mix up their languages so they will not understand each other."*

In the past, there have been many strong languages and attempts to create a common worldwide language. Some worked well, but some not all. The Greek language was used as the "lingua franca" in the days of the Romans. Non-Romans and others read the first Christian books in Greek. Modern Romans speak Italian, but until lately Catholics celebrated Christian ceremonies in Latin, the language of the ancient Romans.

French was the language of upper class Europeans for several hundred years. It was used for international government relations until 1918. Many thought it was clearly the best language for all international communication. Tsarina Catherine of Russia and Frederick the great of Prussia used to speak and write very good French, and made a point to use it with foreigners. A friendly competition took place at the king's court in France in 1853 to find the person who used the best French. The winner was not Emperor Napoleon the Third, or his wife Eugénie. Instead, it was the Austrian statesman Klemens Wenzel von Metternich.

About this time, in the Age of Reason, humans began to think they could do anything. They discovered drugs that would cure diseases. They could grow food in all weather. Their new steam-ships could go anywhere without wind. So then some people thought: **How difficult could it be to create a new language, one that would be easy and useful for all people?**

Technical Words

Chapter - people divide large books into smaller chapters

Dialect - a different way of speaking a mother tongue

Patois - a way of speaking in one region

Lingua franca - a Latin word for a global language

Pronunciation - the way we say sounds when we speak

International Words

Planet - a space globe that moves around the Sun

Chapter 2
Esperanto vs... the World?

Natural languages come from unwritten languages of long ago, in the Stone Age. They are easy to learn naturally but hard to learn as a student. That is why many people have tried to invent a simple language that is useful and simple to learn. Perhaps the most famous of these *invented* languages is "Esperanto." It was developed between 1880 and 1890 by Doctor Ludovic Lazarus Zamenhof. He was a Russian eye doctor in Poland. He said his goal was to create communication and culture-sharing among all the people of the world. He thought the result would be understanding by everyone. That would mean everyone would have sympathy with everyone else and this would avoid future wars.

Here is a example of Esperanto:

> *En multaj lokoj de Ĉinio estis temploj de drako-reĝo. Dum trosekeco oni preĝis en la temploj, ke la drako-reĝo donu pluvon al la homa mondo.*

Easy for you to say… perhaps. But there was one big problem with Esperanto. No one could speak it. Well, not really *no* one.

After more than a century, there are about 3 million people who can speak Esperanto. And that is in a world of nearly 7 *billion* people. Sadly, many wars later, we have to admit the *idea did not work as expected.* For a while, Esperanto was an official project in the USSR, and in the People's Republic of China. It is long

The 1st Esperanto Book by Zamenhof

forgotten in those countries now. There are no Esperanto guides in the Moscow or Shanghai railway stations to help passengers find their trains. We can only wonder what the world would be like if the Soviets had chosen Globish instead...

There are still people who believe in Esperanto. They still have their "special" language. Sometimes Esperantists make news when they speak out against Globish -- using English, of course. Thus any major newspaper story about Globish and Esperanto clearly demonstrates that Esperanto is not working. And it helps show that Globish gives us an opportunity to have – finally – a real global communication tool.

International Words

Million = 1,000,000
Billion = 1,000,000,000

Chapter 3
Thinking Globally

It would be difficult for all people in the world to have one official language. Who would say what that language must be? How would we decide? Who would "own" the language?

Most people today speak only their one national language. This is especially true with native English speakers. They observe that many people in other countries try to speak English. So they think they do not need to learn any other language. It appears to be a gift from their God that they were born ready for international communication. Perhaps, unlike others in the world, they do not have to walk half the distance to communicate with other cultures. Perhaps English IS the place everyone else must come to. Perhaps…. All others are unlucky by birth. But *perhaps* there is more to the story…

It does seem English has won the competition of global communication. Although it used to give people an edge in international business, one observer now states it this way:

"It has become a new baseline: without English you are not even in the race."

So now the competition is over. No other language could be more successful now. Why is that?

The high situation of English is now recognized because communication is now global, and happens in one second. There have been periods in history where one language seemed to have worldwide acceptance. But, in all these periods, the "world" covered by one of these languages was not the whole planet. Chinese was not known to Greeks in the time

of the Roman Empire. The hundreds of Australian languages were not known to Europeans when they settled there. Japanese people did not learn and speak French in the 18th century. Then, much communication was a matter of time and distance. Now, for the first time, communication has no limits on our Earth. 200 years ago it took more than six months to get a message from Auckland, New Zealand, to London. In our global world, a message goes from Auckland to London in less than a second.

As Marshall McLuhan said in his book *The Guttenberg Galaxy*, this world is now just the size of a village – a "global village." In a village, all people communicate in the language of the village. All nations now accept English as the communication for our global village.

Some people dislike that fact a lot. They want to keep their language, and even to avoid English. And, there are people who do not care at all, and they do not see what is happening or what it means. Finally, there are people who accept it, and even benefit from it. Many Chinese, Spanish and German people realize their language is not global and so they are learning English. They speak about their wonderful culture in English but they also continue to speak their first language.

We can be very confident this situation will not change. With all the people now learning English as a second language, and there will be no need to change. As in the past, people will speak more than one language as children.

Leading economic powers, such as China, Brazil, India, Russia, and Japan will have many people speaking English. No one is going to win markets now with military battles.

And no one will need to change languages, as used to happen. Now nations will try to win hearts and minds with their better, less expensive products. It is a new world now, and maybe a better one.

To communicate worldwide, these people will use varying qualities of English. But once they master "a reasonable amount" of English they will not want or need to require others to use their mother tongue. So English will certainly continue to be the most important international language. The economic winners today or tomorrow will use their English well enough so that they don't need anything else. This "common ground" is what everybody will continue to agree on…

Language Used In Business Communication

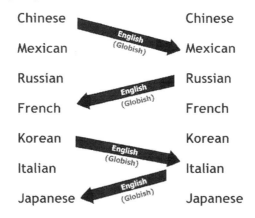

Still, many people will continue to learn Chinese or Spanish or Russian. They will do this to understand other cultures. But it will be of less help in doing worldwide business. In an international meeting anywhere, there will always be people who do not speak the local language. Everyone in this meeting will then agree to change back to English, because everyone there will have acceptable English.

Today, Mandarin Chinese is the language with the most speakers. After that is Hindi, and then Spanish. All three of them have more native speakers than English. But Hindi speakers talk to Chinese speakers in English and Spanish speakers communicate to Japanese speakers in English. They cannot use their own languages so they must use the most international language to do current business. That is why English is now locked into its important position the world over.

Sometimes we wonder if it is good that English won the language competition. We could argue that it is not the right language. It is far too difficult, with far too many words (615,000 words in the Oxford English Dictionary…and they add more each day.) Too many irregular verbs. The grammar is too difficult. And most importantly, English does not have good links between the written and the spoken language. Why do the letters "ough" have four different pronunciations ("cough, tough, though, through") Why is a different syllable stressed in photograph, photography and photographer? And why is there not a stress mark? Why doesn't "Infamous" sound like "famous?" or "wilderness"

Technical

Grammar - the structure of words in a sentence.

Pronounce - to speak accurate sounds in a language

Stress - making a heavy tone on one syllable of a word

Syllable - a part of a word you are saying

Paradox - something that sounds correct but is really the opposite like: *winning is really losing*

Verb - the part of speech that tells the action in a sentence.

International

Pajamas - clothes you wear to bed at night

like "wild?" Why isn't "garbage" pronounced like "garage", or "heathen" like "heather"?

English was never expected to make sense to the ear. **Pronunciation** in English is a horrible experience when you have not been born into that culture. Yet it appears to sound natural to native English speakers.

Some languages, like Italian, German, and Japanese, can match written words to the way they are spoken. So it may appear unlucky for us that one of them did not win it all. Italian, for example, is a language where every letter, and every group of letters, is always *pronounced* the same way. When you are given an Italian document, you can *pronounce* it once you understand a limited number of fixed rules. In English you have to learn the *pronunciation* of every word. Many English words are borrowed from other languages, and they sometimes keep their old pronunciation and sometimes not. English words cannot be written so the stressed syllables are shown. All non-native English speakers know that they may have to sleep without clothes if they try to buy "**pajamas**." Where is the mark to show what we stress in "**pajamas**?" So, the borrowed word "**pajamas**" would be better written as *pa-JA-mas*. In English you must learn exactly which **syllable** gets the **stress**, or *no one* understands you.

But Italian, German, or Japanese did not win the language competition. English did. Luckily, this does not mean that there are people who won and people who lost. In fact, we will show that the people whose language seemed to win did not, in fact, improve their positions. The other people won, and those non-native speakers will soon win even more. This is one of the many "Globish **Paradoxes**."

Chapter 4
The Native Speakers' Edge
is Their Problem

Speaking an extra language is always good. It makes it easier to admit that there are different ways of doing things. It also helps to understand other cultures, to see why they are valued and what they have produced. You can discover a foreign culture through traveling and translation. But truly understanding is another thing: that requires some mastery of its language to talk with people of the culture, and to read their most important books. The "not created here" idea comes from fear and dislike of foreign things and culture. It makes people avoid important ideas and new ways of working.

Native English speakers, of course, speak English most of the time - with their families, the people they work with, their neighbors, and their personal friends. Sometimes they talk to non-native speakers in English, but most English speakers do not do this often. On the other hand, a Portuguese man speaks English most often with non-native English speakers. They all have strange accents. His ears become sympathetic. He learns to listen and understand and not be confused by the accent. He learns to understand a Korean, a Scotsman or a New Zealander with strong local accents. And he learns to understand the pronunciations of others learning English. Often, he understands accents much better than a native English speaker.

It is a general observation that the person who already speaks five languages has very little difficulty learning the sixth one. Even the person who masters two languages is in a much better position to learn a third one than the countryman or countrywoman who sticks only to the mother tongue. That is why it is too bad people no longer speak their local patois. The practice almost disappeared during the 20th century.

Scientists tell us that having a second language seems to enable some mysterious brain connections which are otherwise not used at all. Like muscles with regular exercise, these active connections allow people to learn additional foreign languages more easily.

Now that so many people **migrate** to English-speaking countries, many of the young people in those families quickly learn English. It is estimated, for example, that 10% of all younger persons in the UK still keep another language after they learn English. Probably similar figures are available in the

US. Those children have an extra set of skills when speaking to other new English language learners.

The British Council is the highest authority on English learning and speaking. It agrees with us in its findings. David Graddol of the British Council is the writer of English Next, which is a major study from the British Council. Graddol said (as *translated into Globish*):

> "(Current findings)... should end any sureness among those people who believe that the global position of English is completely firm and protected. We should not have the feeling that young people of the United Kingdom do not need abilities in additional languages besides English."

Graddol confirms:

> "Young people who finish school with only English will face poor job possibilities compared to able young people from other countries who also speak other languages. Global companies and organizations will not want young people who have only English.
>
> Anyone who believes that native speakers of English remain in control of these developments will be very troubled. This book suggests that it is native speakers who, perhaps, should be the most worried. But the fact is that the future

development of English is now a global concern and should be troubling us all.

English speakers who have only English may not get very good jobs in a global environment, and barriers preventing them from learning other languages are rising quickly. The competitive edge (personally, organizationally, and nationally) that English historically provided people who learn it, will go away as English becomes a near-universal basic skill.

English-speaking ability will no longer be a mark of membership in a select, educated, group. Instead, the lack of English now threatens to leave out a minority in most countries rather than the majority of their population, as it was before.

*Native speakers were thought to be the "gold standard" (**idioms remain in this section**); as final judges of quality and authority. In the new, quickly-appearing environment, native speakers may increasingly be indentified as part of the problem rather than being the basic solution. Non-native speakers will feel these "golden"native speakers are bringing along "cultural baggage" of little interest, or as teachers are "gold-plating" the teaching process.*

Traditionally, native speakers of English have been thought of as providing the authoritative standard and as being the best teachers. Now, they may be seen as presenting barriers to the free development of global English.

We are now nearing the end of the period where native speakers can shine in their special knowledge of the global "lingua franca."

Now David Graddol is an expert on this subject. But he is also an Englishman. It would be difficult for him - or any native English speaker - to see all that non-native speakers see... and see differently.

For example, non-native speakers see how native English speakers believe that their pronunciation is the only valid one. Pronunciation is not easy in English. There are versions of English with traditional or old colonial accents. Many different British accents were mixed in the past with local languages in colonies such as America, India, South Africa, Hong Kong, Australia, or New Zealand. Today more accents are becoming common as English gets mixed with the accents from other languages. Learners of English often have to struggle to hear "native" English and then to manage the different accents. Learners often learn English with the older colonial accents or newer accents. Not many people now speak English like the Queen of England.

Also, native speakers often use their local idioms as if they are universal. (Like saying that someone who dies is "biting the dust". How long does it take to explain what these really mean? The modern global citizen does not need language like that.)

Non-native speakers also observe this: that most native speakers believe they are English experts

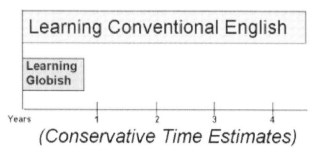

(Conservative Time Estimates)

because they can speak English so easily. Language schools in non-English-speaking countries often have native English speakers as teachers. They are said to be the "gold standard" (an *idiom!*) in English. But these native speakers are not always trained teachers. Often all they have is their ability to pronounce

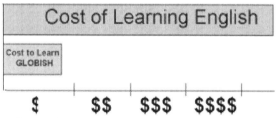

words. They do not know what it is like to learn English. In the end result, a teacher needs to know how to teach. So sometimes non-native English speakers become better teachers of English than people with the perfect UK, or US, or South African English pronunciation.

In the past, English schools have made a lot of money using native speakers to teach English. Thus the students always work towards a goal that is always out of reach. Probably none of these students will ever speak the Queen's English. To achieve that you must be born not far from Oxford or Cambridge. Or, at a minimum, you must have learned English when your voice muscles were still young. That means very early in your life, before 12 years old. Learning to speak without an accent is almost impossible. You will always need more lessons, says the English teacher who wants more work.

But here is the good news: Your accent just needs to be "understandable"...not perfect. Learners of English often need to stop and think about what they are doing. It is wise to remember to ask: how much English do I need? Do I need all the fine words and perfect pronunciation? Perhaps not....

Technical

Idiom - a term for the use of colorful words which may not be understood by non-native speakers.

Lesson - one section of a larger course of study

International

Migrate - to move your home from one country to another. Also: an immigrant is a person who migrates.

31

Chapter 5
The English Learners' Problem...
Can Be Their Edge

Some very expert English speakers take pride in speaking what is called "plain" English. They recommend we use simple English words, and to avoid foreign, borrowed words for example. So speaking plain English is not speaking bad English at all, and might even be speaking rather good English. Using unusual or difficult words does not always mean you know what you are talking about. In many cases, "plain" English is far more useful than other English. The term "Plain English" is the name of a small movement, but the term is most often used between native speakers to tell each other that the subject is too difficult. They say: *"Just tell me in plain English!"*

It is very important, on the other hand, to speak correct English. Correct English means using common English words in sentences that have reasonably good meanings. Of course, everyone makes mistakes now and then, but a good goal is to say things in a correct way using simple words. This makes it easier to say things that are useful.

Of course, we know that we say things well enough if people understand what we say. So we need to observe a level of usage and correctness in English which is "enough" for understanding. Less is not enough. And "more than enough" is too much – too difficult – for many people to understand. Most public messages – such as advertisements use fairly common words and fairly simple English. The messages often cost a lot so it is important everyone understands them. On television, time for messages can cost huge amounts so the English used is chosen very carefully. The American Football Super Bowl in the US has advertisements that are very easy to understand. The advertisers pay $2 000 000 a minute for their advertisements, so they want to be sure people understand!

There is a level of English that is acceptable for most purposes of understanding. This is the level that Globish aims to show. As we will see in greater detail, Globish is a defined subset of English. Because it is limited, everyone can learn the same English words and then they can understand each other. Globish uses simple sentence structures and a small number of words, so that means you have to learn less. And it can be expanded easily when people choose to do this.

The Globish word list has 1500 words. They have been carefully chosen from all the most common words in English. They are listed in the middle of this book. In the Oxford English Dictionary there are about 615000 entries. So how could 1500 words be enough? This book – in Globish – uses those 1500 basic words and their variations.

This list of 1500, of course, will also accept a few other words which are tied to a trade or an industry: call them "**technical** words." (**Technical** is a **technical** word.) Some **technical** words are understood everywhere. In the computer industry, words like web and software are usually known by everyone. They are from English or are made up, like Google. And in the cooking industry, many words are French, like "**sauté**" or "**omelette**".

Globish also uses words that are already international. Travelers communicate using words like "**pizza**", "**hotel**", "**police**", "**taxi**", "**stop**", "**restaurant**", "**toilets**", and "**photo**".

1500 is a lot of words, because English has been a language where words "father" words. The children words of the first 1500 words are easy to learn. For instance, "care" is the father of "careful, carefully, carefulness, careless, carelessly, carelessness, uncaring, caretaker, etc…" It is the same with "use" and hundreds of other words. If you count all the fathers and their children you find over 5,000 Globish words.

Experts say most native English speakers use only about 3,500 words. Well-educated speakers may know many more words but probably only use about 7,500 words. It is demonstrated that even native speakers with high education say 80% of what they have to say with only 20% of their word-wealth. This is only one good example of a universal law called the "Pareto Principle", named after its Paris-born inventor. The Pareto Principle states: For all things that happen, 80% of the results come from 20% of the causes. So, 20% of the educated native speaker's 7500 word wealth is….1500. So with 1500 words, you may communicate better than the average native English speaker , and perhaps as well as the highly-educated one – for 80% of the ideas. For the 20% left over, in Globish you can use a definition instead. You will not say "my nephew", as this could be too difficult in many non-English speaking countries. You will say instead: "the son of my brother". It will be all right.

But where did the 1500 words come from?

Various lists of most-commonly-used English words have suggested the 1500 basic words of Globish. However, the value of a set of words should not be by the place they come from but how well we use them.

On January 20, 2009, Barack Obama made his Presidential Inauguration Speech. Now, in the Appendix of this book, you can see the words he used – alongside Globish words. Take a look at Obama's original speech side-by-side with a version with shorter sentences and only the words of Globish. The non-Globish words that Obama used are marked. You can read the speech in Globish, and decide if Globish can be used to say important things.

Obama's speech in Globish shows that Globish is not poor English. Globish is correct English *and* it can

---

Technical Words

Technical - with a scientific basis, or used by a profession

International Words

Pizza - an Italian food found most places in the world
Hotel - a place to stay which rents many rooms by the night
Police - men or women who make certain you follow the law.
Taxi - a car and driver you rent to take you individual places
Restaurant - a place to eat where you buy single meals
Toilets - places to wash hands and do other necessary things
Photo - a picture taken with a camera
Piano - a large box with many keys to make music with
Sauté - French way of cooking; makes meat or vegetables soft
Omelette - a way of cooking meals with eggs

---

communicate with the greatest number of people all over the world. Of course, native English speakers can understand it very quickly because it is English. And even better: they usually do not notice that it is

Globish. But non-native English speakers *do* see the difference: they understand the Globish better than the English they usually hear from native English speakers.

Chapter 6
The Value of a Middle Ground

There is a story about one of the authors. He worked for an American oil exploration company in his youth. He did not grow up in Oklahoma or Texas like the other workers. One time he had to work with map makers in the high plains of Wyoming. There, the strong winds are always the enemy of communication.

His job was to place recording devices on a long line with the map makers. He would go ahead first with a tall stick, and the oil company map makers behind would sight the stick from far away. They waved at him, to guide him left or right. Then he would shout out the number of the device he planted there, on that straight line. The wind was very loud and he had to shout over it. But often the map makers from Oklahoma and Texas would just shake their heads. They could not understand what he shouted. The boy couldn't talk right – they said.

Then one night, all the men had drinks together. They said they did not want to fire him, but they could not understand his numbers in the wind. After a few more drinks, they decided they could be language teachers. They taught him a new way to count, so the wind would not take away the numbers when he shouted them.

Some of the numbers in the new dialect of English sounded familiar, but others were totally different: (1) "wuhn" (2) "teu" (3) "thray" (4) "foar" (5) "fahve" (6) "seex" (7) "sebn" (8) "ate" (9) "nahne" (10) "teeyuhn" (11) "lebn", and on like that. The map-makers were very happy, and not just because of the drinks. They had saved more than a job. They felt they had saved a soul. They had taught someone to "talk right" as they knew it.

Many people have experiences like this. If we do not speak different languages or dialects, at least we speak differently at times. We can copy different accents. Sometimes we speak in new ways to make it easier for others to understand us, and sometimes to sound like others so we are more like them. We often use different ways of speaking for jokes.

It should be easy to use Globish – the same words for everyone everywhere in the world. One language for everyone would be the best tool ever. It would be a tool for communication in a useful way. It might not be as good for word games as English, or as good for describing deep feelings. But Globish would be much better for communication between – or with – people who are not native English speakers. And, of course, native English speakers could understand it too.

So Globish makes an effective tool. You'll be able to do almost anything with it, with a good understanding of what it is and how it works.

But Globish does not aim to be more than a tool, and that is why it is different from English. English is a cultural language. It is a very rich language. It sometimes has 20 different words to say the same thing. And it has a lot of different ways of using them in long, *long* sentences. Learning all the rest of English is a lifetime of work but there is a good reward. People who learn a lot of English have a rich world of culture to explore. They do a lot of learning and can do a lot with what they learn.

But Globish does not aim so high. It is just meant to be a necessary amount. Globish speakers will enjoy travel more, and can do business in Istanbul, Kiev, Madrid, Seoul, San Francisco and Edinburgh.

This will be worth repeating:

> *Globish is "enough" and less than Globish would be not enough. But more than Globish could be too much, and when you use too much English, many people will not understand you.*

This confuses some people, especially English teachers. They say: "How is better English, richer

English, *not always* better?" English teachers like people to enjoy the language, to learn more and more English. It is their job.

When we see native speakers speak English it seems so easy. We think it should be easy for non-native speakers too. But when we look at English tests, we see that all kinds of English are used. There is no clear level of English, just more and more of it. For example, the TOEIC (Test of English for International Communication) does not tell you when you are ready. It does not say when you have "acceptable" English. Globish is a standard that you can reach. A Globish test can tell you if you have a required amount of language to communicate with other people. That is what brings "understanding" – and either we have it, or we don't.

The British Council says (in Globish again):

> *"For ELF (English as a Lingua Franca) being* <u>*understood*</u> *is most important, rather more important than being perfect. The goal of English – within the ELF idea – is not a native speaker but a good speaker of two languages, with a national accent and some the special skills to achieve understanding with another non-native speaker."*

These non-native speakers, in many cases, speak much less perfect English than native speakers. Speaking with words that go past the words they understand is the best way to lose them. It is better then, to stay within the Globish borders. It is better to do that than to act as if you believe that the best English shows the highest social status. **With Globish, we are all from the same world.**

Chapter 7
The Beginnings of Globish

The *most* important thing about Globish is that it started with non-native English speakers. Some English professor could have said "I will now create Globish to make English easy for these adults who are really children." Then Globish would not be global, but just some English professor's plaything. But the true Globish idea started in international meetings with British, Americans, continental Europeans, and Japanese, and then Koreans. The communication was close to excellent between the British and the Americans. But it was not good between those two and the other people. Then there was a big surprise: the communication between the last three groups, continental Europeans, Japanese, and Koreans, was among the best. There seemed to be one good reason: they were saying things with each other that they would have been afraid to try with the native English speakers – for fear of losing respect. So all of these non-native speakers felt comfortable and safe in what sounded like English, but was far from it.

But those non-native English speakers were all *talking* to each other. Yes, there were many mistakes. And yes, the pronunciation was strange. The words were used in unusual ways. Many native English speakers think English like this is horrible. However, the non-native speakers were enjoying their communication.

But as soon as one of the English or Americans started speaking, everything changed in one second. The non-native speakers stopped talking; most were afraid of speaking to the native English speakers. None of them wanted to say a word that was incorrect.

It is often that way across the world. Non-native English speakers have many problems with English. Some native English speakers say non-natives speak "broken English." In truth, non-native English speakers talk to each other effectively *because* they respect and share the same limitations.

The Frenchman and the Korean know they have similar limitations. They do not use rare, difficult-to-understand English words. They choose words that are "acceptable" because they are the easiest words they both know. Of course, these are not always those of the native speakers, who have so many more words to choose from.

The idea of Globish came from this observation: limitations are not always a problem. In fact, they can be useful, if you understand them. Jean-Paul Nerrière could see that *"if we can make the limitations exactly the same, it will be as if there are no limitations at all".* He decided to record a limited set of words and language that he observed in most non-English speakers. He then suggested that people from various mother tongues can communicate better if they use these carefully chosen limitations. Globish is that "common ground."

Nearly-Identical Limitations Worldwide

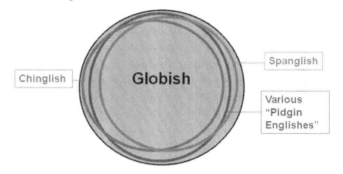

Globish Combines Limitations

This theory of limitations is not as strange as it might seem at first. Most human activities have some limitations.

The World Cup is one of the most-watched competitions in the world, because its set of "limitations" makes it a great game for everyone. In this game of foot-ball, players must use their feet most of the time to control the ball, so tall people and people with big arms do not always win. Some people say it is dancing with the ball; the limitations make it beautiful.

Ballet, of course, has limitations too; it is what you say with your body. And people of every language enjoy both of these. The beauty happens when the limitations are the same. Globish is about having the same limitations, so there is no limit to what can be communicated between people speaking or writing or reading Globish.

We hope the dancers will not start singing in ballets. But what happens when you can use your hands in "foot-ball?" Then – mostly in the English-speaking cultures – we see their American football and Rugby football. These do not have the limitations of playing only with their feet. Not as many people in the world can sit together and enjoy watching. It is not something they all can share, all knowing the same limitations.

The limitations of Globish also make it easier to learn, easier to find a word to use. Native English speakers seem to have too many words that say the same thing and too many ways to say it.

So communication between non-native speakers can be much more effective when they are using Globish. And if non-native and native speakers use Globish between themselves, both of them will understand. Most people would think that native English speakers could know how to speak Globish in one second. But that is not true. Native English speakers who use too many words in too many ways are, in fact, missing a huge opportunity to communicate with the world.

The British Council tells us (here in Globish):

> *"People have wondered for years whether English is so solid in international communication that even the rise of China could not move it from its high position. The answer is that there is already a new language, which was being spoken quietly while native-speakers of English were looking the other way. These native-speakers of English were too happy when they thought their language was the best of all. The new language that is pushing out the language of Shakespeare as the world's Lingua Franca is English itself – English in its new global form. As this book (English Next) shows, this is not English as we have known it, and have taught it in the past as a foreign language. It is a new happening, and if it represents any kind of winning, it will probably not be the cause of celebration by native English speakers."*

The British Council continues (in our Globish):

> *"In organizations where English has become the business language, meetings sometimes go more smoothly when no native speakers are present. Globally, the same kind of thing may be happening, on a larger scale. This is not just because non-native speakers fear to talk to a native*

speaker. The change is that soon the problem may be that few native speakers will be accepted in the community of lingua franca users. The presence of native English speakers gets in the way of communication."

Strangely, many native English speakers still believe they can do all things better than non-native speakers just because they speak better English. How long will it take for them to understand that they are wrong? They have a problem that *they are not able* to understand. They do not see that many non-native speakers simply cannot understand them. This does not mean the native speaker's English is bad. It means that their *communication* is bad; sometimes they do not even attempt to make their communication useful to everyone. Often they don't know how.

We want everyone to be able to speak to and understand everyone. There is a middle ground, but the native English speakers are not the ones drawing the borders. And because you may not be able to say this to a native speaker, who might not be able to understand – we will say it here.

To belong to the international community, a native English speaker must:

- **understand....** what is explained in this book,

- **accept....** that it is the fact of a new world which has many new powers that will be as strong as the English-speaking countries,

- decide **to change** with this new reality, in order to still be a member.

Whenever a native English speaker acts as if *you* are the stupid one, **please give them this book**. If they choose to take no notice of their problem, they will be left out of communication. They will be left out of activities with others – worldwide – if they do not learn to "limit" the way they use their language. English speakers need to limit both spoken and written English for communication with non-native English speakers. In short, they too need to "learn" Globish. It is not an easy exercise, but it can be done. Some of this book will help them.

Globish has a special name

It is very important that the Globish name is *not* "English for the World" or even "Simple English." If its name were *any kind* of English, the native English speakers would say. "OK, we won. Now all you have to do is speak better English." Without the name Globish, they will not understand it is a special kind of English, and it is no longer "their" English. Most native English speakers who understand this should decide they like it. Hopefully they will say: "Now I understand that I am very lucky. Now my language will be changed a little for the rest of the world. Let me do my best, and they can do their best, and we will meet in the middle."

So *Globish* is a word that tells native English speakers – and non-native speakers – that Globish has a different meaning. Globish is the global language, the language people everywhere can speak. Globish is a name to say that there are limits which everyone can learn. There is a clear set of things they need to learn. And when they learn them, they are done.

Language is equal on this Globish middle ground. No one has an edge. No one can be above anyone else because of language. This is the land where everybody can offer the best ideas with all of his or her professional and personal abilities. Globish will be a foreign language to everyone, without exception. It is not "broken English." It is another version of English to which no native English speaker was born.

We all come together here.

Chapter 8
Is Globish More Useful than English?

We talk a lot about international communication, but Globish is also important for *national* communication. In many countries, people speak several languages that are all important. Swiss people speak German, Italian, French or Romansh. Belgians speak French, German, Dutch or Flemish. The largest countries like India, and Russia, and China each have many local languages. Israelis speak Hebrew or Arabic. In many cases, all those people only know their own language. They cannot communicate together because they know only one language; their own. In some countries, even people who *can* speak another language try *not* to speak it. It is the language of a group they do not like.

In all those cases, Globish is the solution. It is much better defined than the "broken English" which is left over from sad school days. Already, in many of these countries, people try to communicate in English just because it is neutral. It is not the language of any one group. Globish is good for them because it offers a solution and is easy to learn.

For people who do not have the time or the money for a full English program, Globish is good. Its plain and simple English will work for them. With Globish they can learn what they need – but no more. They also like the idea of Globish because it is a solution for the person in the street. English, in most cases, is available for educated people, the upper class. In these countries with more than one language, the rich can travel, and the rich can send their children to study in English-speaking countries. The poorest people also need English, to get ahead in their nation and the world, but they do not have the same resources. Globish will allow the people inside nations to talk more, and do more business there and with the rest of the world. That is the result of Globish – more national talk and more global talk.

What makes Globish more inviting is that people can use it very soon. The learners quickly learn some Globish, then more, then most of what they need, and finally all of it. So, Fast Early Progress (FEP) and a Clear End Point (CEP) improve the student's wish to continue. The Return On Effort (ROE) is just as important as ROI (Return On Investment) is for a business person. In fact, they are very much alike.

gl🌐bish

Fast Early Progress (FEP)	+	Clear End Point (CEP)	=	Return On Effort (ROE)
Build on English you have. Globish doesn't need all the kitchen tools, English measures, cultural ideas, or perfect Oxford Pronunciation		*"Enough English" means you can do the most business, travel in the most countries, and talk to the most people, and write to the most people.*		*From "Enough" - each 5% "better" English requires another year of study. All people don't have the time or the money to be more perfect.*

An investor wants to see a valuable return, and a pathway to get there, and a defined end point. In this case, however, every person can be an investor in his or her own future. The average person in the street has valuable skills or ideas that are not being used. If they cannot operate in all of their nation or all of the world, then those skills or ideas have much less value. So we are all investors.

There are several ways to learn Globish. Some learners know about 350 to 500 common words in English and can read and say them. Learning Globish can take these people about 6 months if they study for hour every day, including practice writing and speaking. In six months, with more than 120 days of learning, they can learn just 10 words a day. That should not be too hard.

There may not be a class in Globish near you. However, if you know the limitations given in this book, you can direct a local English teacher to give you only those Globish words and only those Globish sentence structures. *You are the customer*, and you can find English teachers who will do what you ask them to. They do not have to be native-English speakers for you to learn.

Another good thing about this method is that you can start Globish where your last English stopped. If you start Globish knowing 1000 of the most-used English words, then it may take you only 3 *months* to master Globish. That is one of the best things about learning Globish. You know how much to do because you know where it will end.

There are Globish learning materials available. This book – in Globish – has the 1500 words and some other things you need to know. There are a number of materials on Globish already written in local languages or in Globish. There are also computer-based courses, and even a Globish course on a cell phone, the most widely available tool in the world. A lot of written and audio Globish can now be in your pocket or bag.

We should say a few words about pronunciation here. A good teacher can explain how to make clear English sounds. Most teachers will also have audio for you to practice with those sounds. There is a lot of recorded material for learners to practice with. A lot of it is free on the radio, or the World Wide Web. And all of this audio is usually available with the most perfect English accent you can dream of. It can be the Queen's accent. It can be President Obama's accent. It can be whatever you want. Learners should hear different kinds of accents.

You have read here already that a perfect pronunciation is not needed, but only an understandable one, and that is plenty. You must believe this. After all, what is a *perfect accent?* London? Glasgow? Melbourne? Dallas? Toronto? Hollywood? Hong Kong? They *all* think they are perfect! Still, it is widely accepted that only native English speakers can really teach English, and that the teachers with another background should feel like second-class citizens. But this world is changing...quickly.

Before this century, any native English speaker in any non-English-speaking city could sound like he or she knew much more about English, just by pronouncing English quickly and correctly. Non-native English teachers were sometimes worried that they were not well-qualified. They worried that people would discover their English was not perfect. There is good news now. Those days are gone. The old ideas might have been correct about English teaching in the year

1900, but not now. This is a new century. And Globish is the new language in town.

If you are such a teacher of English, things will change for you… all to the better.

If you are such a teacher: welcome to a world that really wants what you can do.

Chapter 9
A Tool and... A Mindset

Globish can achieve what it does because it is useful English *without* a huge number of words and cultural idioms. If Globish speakers can use just this middle level of English, they will be respected everywhere in the world. But the most important difference between English and Globish is how we think when we use Globish.

Who is responsible for effective communication? Is it the speaker and writer, or the listener and reader? The listener and reader cannot make communication good if the speaker or writer does not help. Who is guilty if the message does not get across? Who should do everything possible to make sure he or she is understood?

In English, the usual native speaker would answer: "Not me. I was born with English as a mother tongue, and I started listening to it – and learning it – in my mother's arms. If you do not understand me, it is your prolem. My English is perfect. When yours gets better, you will not have the same difficulty. If you lack the drive to learn it, this is your problem, and not mine. English is the most important language. I am not responsible for that, but there is nothing I can do to make it different."

Globish is the complete opposite: the person who wants to talk must come at least half the distance to the person he talks to. He or she must decide what is necessary to make the communication happen. The native English speaker or the excellent speaker of English as a second language must say: "Today I must speak at the Globish level so this other person can understand me. If my listeners do not understand me, it is because I am not using the Globish tool very well. This is my responsibility, not theirs." Of course, not everyone accepts the idea of Globish yet. Perhaps they never heard about it. Perhaps they could never find the time to learn about it. Or perhaps they did not think they needed it.

Even if there are just two people, if this communication is important, Globish will help. This means you – the speaker – will take responsibility, using simple Globish words in a simple way, and using Globish "best practices" including body language and charts or pictures we can see. Most of all, when using Globish, the speaker should to wait for the listeners, to check they understand.

If there is a group of people, maybe only one does not speak Globish. The speaker can think: "This person is the only one in the group who can not understand or communicate in Globish. That is too bad. I will ask one of the others to help that one by explaining what was said in this discussion."

So sometimes we decide it is better to communicate with those who understand, and let them tell any others. This means it is good to stop now and then, so the other persons can learn what was said. The English speakers will understand anyway, and the below-Globish level will not at all, but you must work with the identified Globish group until you succeed. If you do not communicate with those, the failure will be yours.

On the other hand, there will be times when you are with native English speakers who do not know about the Globish guidelines, never heard of them, or just don't want to hear about it. But it is up to you to bring the discussion to the correct level. This is in your best interest, but it is also your duty, because many of the members of this group may already be lost in this discussion.

You must now be their Globish leader. They will be more than thankful to you for bringing the matter into the open without fear. It is easy. Many English speakers forget about others or just do not think about them. You just have to raise a hand, wave it until you are noticed, and say: "Excuse me, I am sorry but some of us do not understand what you are saying. We need to understand you. Could you please repeat, in Globish please, this time?"

To be sure, you will have a reaction, and your native-speaker friend might understand the point for the rest of his or her life. You will have done a great service. But the first reaction is most likely going to be surprise: "Globish, what's that?" It will give you a fine opportunity to explain the story you now understand, and give its reasons. At best you will have an interested native speaker, who wants to know more, will understand your explanation, and will become a much better global communicator, and a Globish friend. That person will see that Globish is often better than English because it is much more sympathetic.

As we said, pronunciations are "acceptable" as soon as they are understood. A foreign accent is never a mistake; it is part of a person's special quality. It makes you different, and can even make you sound sexy. People who have reasonable Globish pronunciation can now stop trying to make it "better" – or to get closer to some native English speaker's – if they are understood.

We said Globish is still correct English. This means you are expected to write and speak in correct English. The grammar should be reasonable –about subjects and actions, time and place. Globish does not worry about very small differences in American and British speech or spelling or grammar. (And neither should anyone else.)

Globish is much more forgiving because it is asking for understanding, not perfect English. But there is an extra benefit in Globish to all native and non-native speakers: simplicity. It is what older politicians tell younger politicians about their first speeches. It is what older advertising people tell the bright younger ones about making a successful advertisement. It is what news editors tell their young writers about making a good news story. And it is what every English speaking professor should tell every non-native English student about writing and speaking.

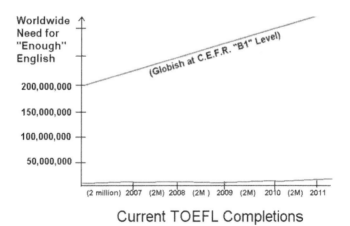

Current TOEFL Completions

On one side of the ocean, Winston Churchill said: "Never use a pound (£) word when a penny (1d) one will do"....

And a similar saying known to Americans:

K. I. S. S. = Keep It Simple, Stupid.

Chapter 10
Globish in Many Places

Globish has no desire to be a cultural language like French, or Chinese...or English. People who will use Globish already have their own respected culture and their own language. They will use Globish only as a tool, but it will be the chosen tool of a huge majority of people around the world. When they see ahead to this future many non-native English speakers will decide this is still English. And it is really a form of English, a clear form of that language. They may fear that English is winning over everything they love. They may see this as a threat to their own mother tongue and their culture. So they might decide that they have to fight for the survival of their French, Japanese, Russian or Tagalog – their home and beloved language. Each of them is a respected cultural language for many people.

This threat could be true IF we were advising you to learn English. That would be helping English compete with other cultural languages. A few cultures have already taken extreme steps because they fear that the English culture will replace their own. They feel it brings poor values and takes away the strength of their own culture.

However, advising you to learn Globish does the opposite. Globish cannot have any cultural goals, so it does not threaten anyone's language or anyone's culture. It replaces the English competition. Using only Globish could keep all these wonderful cultures *safer* from the English cultural invasion.

Globish can also protect the English language from being "broken" by other cultures. English is a very special case today. In fact, the non-native English speakers who use English are far more numerous than native English speakers. So the non-native speakers will decide and lead in the future of the English language. They will create and present new words, and will throw away the old words. This will happen unless the Globish idea becomes an accepted tool. If this happens, it will give the English language a chance to survive as a cultural language.

Globish offers the English-speaking countries a chance to say: We have a wonderful language, linked to a wonderful culture, and we would like to save all of that. However, we accept that international communication today is mostly using our language. But we can divide the language in two parts. One form will be for English culture that is ours, and one form will be for global communication, trade, and traveling (and this is Globish, with exact rules.) We will attempt to use this second form - Globish - whenever we are in those other worlds which are not part of the English culture (s). And we are the lucky ones...Learning Globish for us will be much easier than learning a new language for each place.

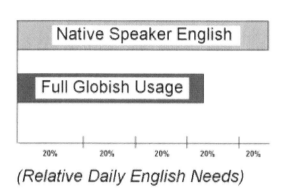

(Relative Daily English Needs)

If you are delivering a speech in front of a large international audience, you have to deal with many different levels of English. You might think they are like one person, but each individual has different abilities. On top of that, someone will be recording you, and your performance will be available in many ways, including on the TV and on the Internet and on DVDs. You need to be understood quickly by the largest possible number. You might think that excellent speakers of two languages are the answer. **Interpreters** give second-by-second changes to the audience in their languages. But even that method is much better with Globish than with English. The Globish limitations and especially its simpler sentences, shorter and lighter, all ensure better correctness when the speech is changed to another language.

Ask any **interpreter**: Their worst experience is the long, involved sentences where they get lost. This person needs to listen to all of the words to get the meaning, and if the talk is too long, he or she has lost the beginning when the end finally comes. But those kinds of statements-within-statements are mistakes in Globish.

The other horrible experience of the **interpreters** is seeing words used differently in a field or subject that they don't know. In English there is the word "program", and it means very different things on the TV and on the computer. The **interpreter** who does not know the field completely will make too many mistakes. On the other hand, if you are talking in Globish, many people in the audience will choose to listen directly to you. The simplest solution is to say things in Globish. You can then use special "technical words" – along with pictures to support them – in a way that people in the industry will quickly understand.

It is very difficult to use Globish guidelines while you are creating your words right there in front of people. But once you are familiar with the idea, practice makes it easier within a short time. The safest way, however, is to give a speech from a written text, and go over that text with Globish software. It will improve the "hit rate" of the speech (a technical term for the percent of people who listen and do understand). Usually it is at least three times better, and ten times with some listeners who are *not* native English speakers.

A good example is the excellent video tape to the Iranian people by President Obama in 2009. It was in Globish-like language and it could be understood by much of the world without translation. They also listened to Obama's same words in Jerusalem and Ramallah, in Istanbul and in Seoul. In too many other cases, however, major international speeches are made at a level of English that is too difficult for non-native speakers. Of course those international speakers think they did their job. They are wrong. Their job was to be understood by all their listeners.

If you are a native English speaker, you could argue that things are very different when you write. You know who you are writing to, and you know that his or her English is very good. Perhaps you write to that person with difficult words to show your ability with the language. But this could be another huge mistake. Very often good ideas are passed on as is to others. You should know that whatever you write today is not written just for the person you send it to. It is always written for the whole wide world. And for this reason, it should be in Globish. If it is forwarded through the Internet it can go around the world 4000 times before you finish your next call. The problem is, if they don't understand it, they will still try to pick up a few words and tell that to their friends. And then what you didn't say well they will say even more poorly in 5000 other languages. The good news is that now you can talk to the whole world at the speed of light. But the really bad news is that no one will ever tell you they don't understand. They would be ashamed to show their limitations, so they will all say back to you: "Oh yes, it was very interesting."

You could be working for a global company, with shares owned by people from 123 different countries. They speak almost as many languages. Look closely at your yearly report, and at all the papers sent to shareholders. It is probably written in wonderful English which non-native English speakers from the 117 non-English speaking countries can almost understand. Or is it written in Globish, using exactly the same numbers and saying exactly the same things, but understandable by many more of those shareholders?

If you work in a government agency in an English speaking country, look at the papers and forms for the citizens. Many people –who are new to the country and to your language – will have to fill in those forms. They should reach the Globish level soon, and that may be fairly easy. But then, they should get papers written only in Globish, which are understandable *both* by these new ones *and* by all the English-speaking citizens. It would cost much less than printing every paper and form in many different languages. And new people could perform better and more quickly in the economy if they could read the language. Globish can fill this need, but that nation must make this standard, and demonstrate it in all its important papers.

There will always be a few of the new people who cannot yet operate in Globish, even to read simple writing. They may still need to see something in their languages. From normal English the usual solution would be many translators, one for each language. Their work might be excellent, but it would take a lot of time and a lot of money.

You could also decide to have computer **translations** to these languages from English. But you must make sure that it works; here is how to do that. Have the computer **translate** part of your English version into – say – Poldevian. When you have a result, do not show it immediately to the Poldevians. Instead, order the computer to change the Poldevian document back to English. If you think you can understand it – and accept it – then the process is good. In most cases you will be surprised in a bad way. You will decide that computers cannot change languages very well yet. However, Globish has a much better chance of giving good results in computer translation. It has simpler sentence structures, and uses the most common English words. Many times, the computer **translation** from Globish to Poldevian will give better results, but not perfect results. This is true of most of Globish, where the goal is to create understanding without 100% perfection.

We must remember, however, that Globish is not a holy language. It is an idea, a guidance. The better you keep to it, the more people will understand you. Perhaps it is like a diet. The closer you stay to it, the more weight you lose. But no diet is going to fail if – just a few times – you have a glass of wine, or a beer. Off-limits words in Globish are not wrong; it is just not wise to bring in difficult words too often. You can use a rare word because no other one will do, and many readers will run to their word books. Or you can use two Globish words that are widely understood by your readers or listeners... and mean the same thing. It is up to you. But the more you stay with the guidance, the better chance you have of everyone understanding you.

It is clear also that people who decide to use Globish will possibly master many more words than the list given here. This is clearly true for advanced English students, of course, but also for the other speakers. In many cases the non-native speakers will hear speech or see written material that uses more difficult words.

In most cases, non-native speakers will learn these new words, and have them available in case they need to use them again later. This is a good result. We are not suggesting that people close their eyes and their ears to all new words. And there will often be native English speakers who reject the Globish idea completely. With this kind of people, more words will always help the non-native speakers to understand.

But these borders of this Globish "middle ground" are not made to keep people in or out. If all speakers know they can come back and be welcomed into Globish, then communication has a chance.

Technical Words

Interpreter - a person who tells the meaning in one language to those who speak another language.

Translation - Changing of one language to another. Sometime human translators are called interpreters as well.

Part 2

Elements of Globish

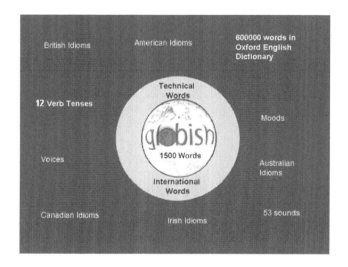

(1500 words, 6-10 verb-time formations, phrasal verbs, 8 parts of speech, plus Active, Passive, Conditional forms. Best: 15-word sentences, Maximum 26 word sentences)

Chapter 11
How much is "enough"?

Globish is "enough" English. That is why a person can learn it more quickly than full English. There are many structures, rules, and ways of using English which make it difficult. Globish has limits so that it is easier to learn and start speaking. A person can know exactly *what* to learn. This is also very helpful in communication between people of varying English abilities. They can all know what to say and write.

But the question will always be asked: "What does "enough" mean? What is "enough?" "Not enough" means that you cannot communicate comfortably with anyone, in English or Globish. You may not know enough words or – more likely – you do not say words with the right stresses, or you may not know simple sentence forms and verb forms. So how much is "too much?" "Too much" makes many students learning English feel they will "never be good enough" in English.

The Council of Europe offers a *Common European Framework of Reference for Languages* (C.E.F.R.) that offers a situational test for users of all second languages. By their standard, the best user of Globish would be an Independent User (Their category called "B1") THIS IS GIVEN EXACTLY IN C.E.F.R.'s ENGLISH:

> *Can understand the main points of clear standard input on familiar matters regularly encountered in work, school, leisure, etc. Can deal with most situations likely to arise whilst travelling in an area where the language is spoken.*

> *Can produce simple connected text on topics, which are familiar, or of personal interest. Can describe experiences and events, dreams, hopes & ambitions and briefly give reasons and explanations for opinions and plans.*

That is the test for "enough" for their B1 - Independent User. It would be enough for the Globish user too, if we added this:

> *"Uses all words needed to join in a given profession or activity; uses International words appropriate in all travel or international business situations."*

But many Globish users can operate at the higher Level B2 of that same C.E.F.R. Independent User standard:

> *"Can understand the main ideas of complex text on both concrete and abstract topics, including technical discussions in his/her field of specialisation. Can interact with a degree of*

fluency and spontaneity that makes regular interaction with native speakers quite possible without strain for either party. Can produce clear, detailed text on a wide range of subjects and explain a viewpoint on a topical issue giving the advantages and disadvantages of various options."

So there are people who have been thinking about this Globish "level" of language use. There are many, many more who have been using something quite close to Globish. Even with few written standards, some have called it Globish because they feel their level of usage is "Globish." They are using the word "Globish" to establish a level of comfort - a middle ground to communicate with others. Now we hope they can be even more certain because of the observations in this book.

At the risk of saying some important things once again, we will now unite some observations from the first part of the book. This will lay the groundwork for describing major language elements that are important to Globish.

First we will review the ways Globish is like English and then how Globish differs from English. Then, we will examine what makes this Closed System of Natural Language an effective tool for world communication.

English speakers may well say: If Globish is like English, why not just learn English? But there are certain things English speakers do not try to understand. That is one of the main reasons people in many places will be speaking Globish.

Chapter 12
Is Globish the Same as English?

Globish is correct English

Native English speakers can easily read and understand this book. But because of this, English speakers do not always notice that Globish is not just **any** English. They can miss the value of limiting their English to Globish. It should instead be a comfort to them, that what they are reading can also be easily understood by Globish speakers as well.

In reading this book, all English-speakers are observing a "common ground" *in action*. Most probably as many as one and a half billion other people can read and understand this same book.

Of course, at first it might seem that all English speakers can use Globish almost without thinking. However, English speakers who want to speak and write Globish must do four things: (1) use short sentences; (2) use words in a simple way; as any advertiser or politician knows. (3) use only the most common English words, and (4) help communication with body language and **visual** additions. Also, they must find ways to repeat what they decide is very important.

Globish spelling is English spelling

Most English speakers have trouble with their own spelling, because the English words come from many cultures. There are probably more exceptions to the rules than there are rules. Often, people learn to spell English words by memory: they *memorize* what the word *looks like*.

Globish sounds like English

Globish speakers must learn to stress parts of words correctly. If the stress is correct, the word is most easily understood. It does not matter so much about the accent.

Technical Words:

Capitalize - put a large letter at the first of the word.

Visual - can be seen with the eyes

Tenses - the time a verb shows, Present, Past, or Future order.

Voice - a type of grammar. We use Active voice most in Globish.

Moods - ways of speaking. Imperative Mood: *"Don't look at me!"*

And some sounds that are hard to make do not matter so much. A second problem in pronunciation is easier: the *schwa* sound can often be substituted in most parts of words that are *not* stressed. (More in Chapters 16 and 21).

Globish uses the same letters, markings and numbers as English

It also has the same days, months and other time and place forms.

Globish uses the basic grammar of English, with fewer Tenses, Voices, and Moods.

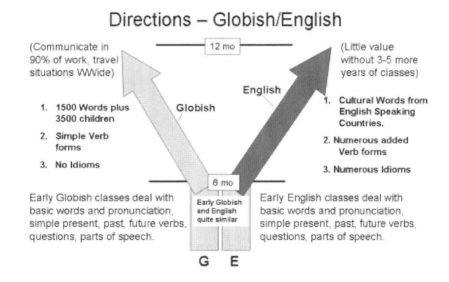

Directions – Globish/English

(Communicate in 90% of work, travel situations WWide)

12 mo

(Little value without 3-5 more years of classes)

English

Globish

1. 1500 Words plus 3500 children

2. Simple Verb forms

3. No Idioms

1. Cultural Words from English Speaking Countries.

2. Numerous added Verb forms

3. Numerous Idioms

6 mo

Early Globish and English quite similar

Early Globish classes deal with basic words and pronunciation, simple present, past, future verbs, questions, parts of speech.

Early English classes deal with basic words and pronunciation, simple present, past, future verbs, questions, parts of speech.

G   E

Chapter 13
How Globish is Different from English

Globish has a different name

The name lets people know exactly how much English they are using. It also lets native English speakers know that they do not "own" this language. Globish means we use the same simple rules for everyone. And it usually means that the speaker or writer is trying to help with understanding. Globish speakers enjoy the fact that all cultures are talking *together*.

Globish has 1500 words, expandable in four ways:

- different use of same word,
- combinations of words,
- short additions to words,
- and Phrasal Verbs.

Also allowed are (a) Names and Titles - (**capitalized**), (b) international words like *police* and *pizza*, (c) technical words like *noun* and *grammar* in this book. Only common agreement between speakers can decide between them, of course, what other words to allow beyond these 1500 Globish words. If one person cannot understand an additional word, then its use is not recommended. (See Chapters 16 and 17)

Globish uses mostly Active Voice

Globish speakers should understand Passive and Conditional forms. But it is usually best for Globish users to create messages in Active Voice if possible. Who or what is doing the action must be clear in Globish. English may say:

> *The streets were cleaned in the morning.*

But Globish would say (See Chapter 18):

> *The workmen cleaned the streets in the morning.*

Globish suggests short sentences (15 words or fewer)

This limits phrases and clauses, but allows them if necessary. Instead of:

> *When we went to Paris we took a nice little hotel not far from the main shopping area so that we would not have too far to carry our purchases.*

Globish speakers will say:

We went to Paris, and we found a nice little hotel. It was near the main shopping area. That way, we would not have too far to carry our purchases.

Globish pronunciation has fewer necessary sounds than traditional English

Globish sounds should be learned with each word. Most important: Globish must use syllable stress VEry corRECTly. Because there are similar sounds in most languages, each speaker may have to learn only a few new sounds. (See Chapter 21).

Globish speakers use their body, their hands and their face when they talk

They use headlines, **dark print**, <u>underline</u>, and pictures with written Globish. In meetings, Globish speakers use objects, pictures, sounds, and give things to the listeners. Good Globish speakers speak clearly, and are happy to repeat what they have said. Globish speakers check that the listeners understand before they say the next thing. They repeat all questions AND answers in meetings. (More in Chapter 18)

Globish speakers are very careful about humor, idioms and examples

Globish speakers can have fun, and be friendly. But they avoid anything that might not be understood. Most people are careful not to use the same humor with their parents and their friends. Sometimes humor is good for one person but offensive to another. This is even more difficult to know about between cultures, so it is best to avoid trying to be "funny". In the same way, examples from one culture might not be good in another culture and some analogies might not carry exactly the same meaning. And idioms, things that depend on understanding a certain culture, should be avoided. (More in Chapter 19)

> **Technical words**
>
> Noun - a part of speech naming a person, place, or thing.
>
> Passive Voice - a sentence with no subject. "The house is sold."
>
> Active Voice - usual sentence - subject first. "Mary came home."
>
> Figurative - expressing one thing in terms of another: "on thin ice."
>
> Analogy - using two things that have a similarity to make a case.
>
> *Analogy*: "The human brain is like a computer."

Globish is a "Closed System of Natural Language."

This is what makes Globish useful, dependable, and easier to learn and use. The next chapters will be about "natural language" and Globish's closed system.

Chapter 14
Natural Language Has "Experience"

People need a language that has "experience". We need to know other people have lived all their lives talking in that language. We need to know that many centuries, many parents and their children, have made it work well. Natural language is always growing. The "closed system" of Globish, of course, is a beginning definition. Over time, Globish may add necessary words as *technical* or *international* when worldwide Globish speakers are using it.

The value of having a natural language is because it has been tested with many millions of people. Its most-used words have been turned over and over, like sand on a seaside, for centuries. These words are the *survivors* from all the natural languages that came into English. They are strong words, and useful words.

And these rules of Globish are not something someone just "thought up." For example, the way English deals with time through its verbs. Now all languages have different ways of communicating the order of happenings. But as much as any language, English-speakers have a proven language where events have relationships to each other in time. So timing is important to the English way of thinking, important to their communication. If they want to say something is happening "now" they use a continuous form, such as *I am reading this book*. That Present Continuous form means "exactly now." If they say *I read this book*, it means they have read it before now, are reading it now, and will continue to read it in the future.

These things are all important to a "way of thinking." They don't happen by someone's plan. Natural Language grows through trial-and-mistake-and-improvement, and that is why Natural Language works!

But why do we call Globish a "Closed System?" And is "closed" good?

Chapter 15
A Closed System: Globish Limitations

Closed Systems give us less to remember, and more to agree on

"Closed System" means we accept certain sets of limitations in what we are doing. It makes life easier when we agree to operate within those Closed Systems. We also have many other Closed Systems. Buses and trains and airplanes usually have places to step on and off. We usually drive on just one side of the road. Cars coming the other way stay on the other side, because it is a closed system. Otherwise, either side of the road would be OK, and there would be huge problems.

So.... why can't a language be a Closed System?

This is why Globish is most useful, as a Closed System, a language built on common limitations. You know what you have to learn, and can do so with less effort. And when you use it, you know all the rules that the other people know. It is based on reasonable limitations that non-native English speakers have when they use English. What we have been discussing in this book are main elements of that Closed System:

Globish is limited to 1500 words

Globish has limited ways of using words.

Globish has limited length sentences.

Globish is limited to understanding.

Globish has no limits in using hands, face, or body.

Chapter 16
1500 Basic Words

Before the English teachers all ask one question, let us answer it. There is *no* evidence that having 1500 words is ideal, except for one thing: *It's easier to learn 1500 words than 1800 or 2000 words.* And with fewer than 1000 words you won't have some very common words when you need them. Also, you can learn spelling and pronunciation of each individual word. That way you won't have to worry about a lot of spelling and pronunciation rules. (You probably already know that English doesn't do well with its spelling and pronunciation rules.)

These 1,500 words come from several lists of most-commonly used English words. It is very much like the 1500 words used by Voice of America, but it has fewer political words. It is very much like basic Technical English used in international training books but without all of words for measurements. In fact, there are many lists of the "most common" 1500 words, and they all vary a lot in the last 200 words, depending on who is selecting. **So this is ours.**

The Basic 1500 Globish Words:

a	air	area	bag	best	border
able	alive	argue	balance	betray	born
about	all	arm	ball	better	borrow
above	allow	army	ballot	between	boss
accept	ally	around	ban	big	both
according(to)	almost	arrest	bank	bill	bottle
account	alone	arrive	bar	bird	bottom
accuse	along	art	barrier	birth	box
achieve	already	as	base	bit	boy
across	also	ask	basket	bite	boycott
act	although	assist	bath	black	brain
adapt	always	at	battle	blade	brake
add	among	attach	be	blame	branch
admit	amount	attack	bear	blank	brave
adult	and	attempt	beat	blanket	bread
advertisement	anger	attend	beauty	bleed	break
advise	angle	attention	because	blind	breathe
affect	announce	authority	become	block	brick
afraid	another	automatic	bed	blood	bridge
after	answer	autumn	beer	blow	brief
again	any	available	before	blue	bright
against	apartment	average	begin	board	bring
age	apologize	avoid	behind	boat	broad
agency	appeal	awake	believe	body	broadcast
ago	appear	award	bell	bomb	brother
agree	apple	away	belong	bone	brown
ahead	apply	baby	below	bonus	brush
aid	appoint	back	bend	book	budget
aim	approve	bad	beside	boot	build

bullet
burn
burst
bury
business
busy
but
butter
button
buy
by
cabinet
call
calm
camera
camp
campaign
can
cancel
capture
car
card
care
carriage
carry
case
cash
cat
catch

cause
celebrate
cell
center
century
ceremony
certain
chain
chair
chairman
challenge
champion
chance
change
channel
character
charge
chart
chase
cheap
check
cheer
cheese
chemical
chest
chief
child
choose
church

circle
citizen
city
civilian
claim
clash
class
clean
clear
climate
climb
clock
close
cloth
cloud
coal
coast
coat
code
cold
collect
college
colony
color
combine
come
comfort
command
comment

committee
common
communicate
community
company
compare
compete
complete
compromise
computer
concern
condemn
condition
conference
confirm
congratulate
congress
connect
consider
consumption
contact
contain
continent
continue
control
cook
cool
cooperate
copy

cork
corn
corner
correct
cost
cotton
count
country
course
court
cover
cow
crash
create
credit
crew
crime
crisis
criteria
criticize
crop
cross
crowd
crush
cry
culture
cup
cure
current

custom
cut
damage
dance
danger
dark
date
daughter
day
dead
deaf
deal
dear
debate
debt
decide
declare
decrease
deep
defeat
defend
define
degree
delay
delicate
deliver
demand
demonstrate
denounce

deny	distance	edge	especially	export*	fight
departure	divide	education	establish	express	figure
depend	do	effect	estimate	extend	file
deploy	doctor	effort	ethnic	extra	fill
depression	document	egg	evaporate	extreme	film
describe	dog	either	even	eye	final
desert*	door	elastic	event	face	finance
design	doubt	electricity	ever	fact	find
desire	down	element	every	factory	fine
destroy	drain	else	evidence	fail	finger
detail	draw	embassy	evil	fair	finish
develop	dream	emergency	exact	fall	fire
device	dress	emotion	example	false	firm
die	drink	employ	except	family	first
diet	drive	empty	exchange	famous	fish
differ	drop	end	excuse	far	fist
difficult	drug	enemy	execute	fast	fit
dig	dry	enforce	exercise	fat	fix
dinner	during	engine	exist	father	flag
diplomat	dust	enjoy	exit	fear	flat
direct	duty	enough	expand	feather	float
dirt	each	enter	expect	feature	floor
disappear	ear	entertain	expense	feed	flow
discover	early	environment	experience	feel	flower
discuss	earn	equal	experiment	female	fluid
disease	earth	equate	expert	fertile	fly
disk	east	equipment	explain	few	fog
dismiss	easy	erase	explode	field	fold
dispute	eat	escape	explore	fierce	follow

96

food	gang	**gui**lty	hill	**hur**ry	**in**sect
fool	**gar**den	gun	him	hurt	ins**pect**
foot	gas	guy	hire	**hus**band	ins**tead**
for	**gat**her	hair	his	I	**in**sult*
for**bid**	**gen**eral	half	**his**tory	ice	**in**surance
force	**gen**tle	halt	hit	i**dea**	in**tel**ligence
foreign	get	hand	hold	i**den**tify	in**tense**
forest	gift	hang	hole	if	**in**terest
for**get**	girl	**hap**pen	**hol**iday	ill	inter**fere**
for**give**	give	**hap**py	**hol**low	i**ma**gine	international
form	glass	hard	**hol**y	**im**port*	**in**to
former	**glob**al	harm	home	im**por**tant	in**vade**
forward	go	hat	**hon**est	im**prove**	in**vent**
frame	goal	hate	hope	in	in**vest**
free	god	have	**hor**rible	inch	in**ves**tigate
freeze	gold	he	horse	**in**cident	in**vite**
fresh	good	head	**hos**pital	in**clude**	in**volve**
friend	**gov**ern	heal	**hos**tage	in**crease***	iron
frighten	grass	health	**hos**tile	independent	**is**land
from	gray (grey)	hear	hot	**in**dicate	**is**sue
front	great	heart	hour	indi**vi**dual	it
fruit	green	heat	house	**in**dustry	**it**em
fuel	ground	**hea**vy	how	in**fect**	**jack**et
full	group	help	**how**ever	**in**fluence	jail
fun	grow	her	huge	in**form**	**jew**el
future	**gua**rantee	here	**hum**an	in**ject**	job
gain	guard	hide	**hum**or	**in**jure	join
gallon	guess	high	**hun**ger	**in**nocent	joint
game	guide	**hi**jack	hunt	in**sane**	joke

97

joy	lead	load	**mas**ter	miscellaneous	**na**rrow
judge	leak	loan	match	miss	**na**tion
jump	learn	**lo**cal	material	mis**ta**ke	**na**tive
jury	least	lo**cate**	**mat**ter	mix	**na**vy
just	leave	lock	may	mob	near
keep	left	log	**may**or	**mod**el	**ne**cessary
key	leg	lone	me	**mod**erate	neck
kick	**le**gal	long	meal	**mod**ern	need
kid	lend	look	mean	**mon**ey	**neigh**bor
kill	length	loose	**mea**sure	month	**nei**ther
kind	less	lose	meat	moon	nerve
king	let	lot	**me**dia	**mor**al	**neu**tral
kiss	**let**ter	loud	meet	more	**nev**er
kit	**lev**el	love	**mem**ber	**morn**ing	new
kitchen	lie	low	**me**mory	most	news
knife	lie	luck	**men**tal	**moth**er	next
know	life	mail	**mer**cy	**mo**tion	nice
labor	lift	main	**mes**sage	**moun**tain	night
laboratory	light	**ma**jor	**met**al	mouth	no
lack	like	make	**met**hod	move	noise
lake	**li**mit	male	**mid**dle	much	noon
land	line	man	might	**mur**der	**nor**mal
language	link	manu**fac**ture	mile	**mus**cle	north
large	lip	**ma**ny	**mil**itary	**mus**ic	nose
last	**li**quid	map	milk	must	not
late	list	march	mind	my	note
laugh	**lis**ten	mark	mine	**mys**tery	**noth**ing
law	**lit**tle	**mar**ket	**min**ister	nail	**no**tice
lay	live	**mar**ry	**mi**nor	name	now

nowhere	ounce	pen	pocket	private	question
number	our	pencil	point	prize	quick
obey	ours	people	poison	problem	quiet
object	oust	percent	policy	process	quit
observe	out	perfect	politics	product	quite
occupy	over	perform	pollute	professor	race
occur	owe	perhaps	poor	profit	radiation
of	own	period	popular	program	raid
off	page	permanent	port	progress*	rail
offensive	pain	permit	position	project*	rain
offer	paint	person	possess	property	raise
office	pan	physical	possible	propose	range
officer	pants	pick	postpone	protect	rare
often	paper	picture	potato	protest	rate
oil	parade	piece	pound	prove	rather
old	parcel	pig	pour	provide	ray
on	parent	pilot	powder	public	reach
once	parliament	pint	power	publish	react
only	part	pipe	practice	pull	read
open	party	place	praise	punish	ready
operate	pass	plain	pray	purchase	real
opinion	passenger	plan	pregnant	pure	reason
opportunity	past	plane	present	purpose	receive
opposite	paste	plant	press	push	recognize
oppress	path	plastic	pretty	put	record*
or	patient	plate	prevent	quality	recover
order	pattern	play	price	quart	red
organize	pay	please	print	quarter	reduce
other	peace	plenty	prison	queen	refugee

refuse*	reward	sail	senate	shoe	slave
regret	rice	salt	send	shoot	sleep
regular	rich	same	sense	shop	slide
reject	ride	sand	sentence	short	slip
relation	right	satisfy	separate	should	slow
release	ring	save	series	shout	small
remain	riot	say	serious	show	smart
remember	rise	scale	serve	shrink	smash
remove	risk	scare	set	shut	smell
repair	river	school	settle	sick	smile
repeat	road	science	several	side	smoke
report	rob	score	severe	sign	smooth
represent	rock	script	sex	signal	snack
request	rocket	sea	shade	silence	snake
require	roll	search	shake	silk	sneeze
rescue	roof	season	shall	silver	snow
research	room	seat	shame	similar	so
resign	root	second	shape	simple	soap
resist	rope	secret	share	since	social
resolution	rough	section	sharp	sing	society
resource	round	security	she	single	soft
respect	row	see	sheet	sister	soil
responsible	rub	seed	shelf	sit	soldier
rest	rubber	seek	shell	situation	solid
restrain	ruin	seem	shelter	size	solve
result	rule	seize	shine	skill	some
retire	run	seldom	ship	skin	son
return	sad	self	shirt	skirt	song
revolt	safe	sell	shock	sky	soon

sorry	steal	sudden	talk	they	tool
sort	steam	suffer	tall	thick	tooth
soul	steel	sugar	target	thin	top
sound	step	suggest	task	thing	total
south	stick	suit	taste	think	touch
space	still	summer	tax	third	toward
speak	stomach	sun	tea	this	town
special	stone	supervise	teach	those	track
speech	stop	supply	team	though	trade
speed	store	support	tear	thought	tradition
spell	storm	suppose	tear	threaten	traffic
spend	story	suppress	tell	through	train
spirit	straight	sure	term	throw	transport*
spot	strange	surface	terrible	thus	travel
spread	stream	surprise	territory	tie	treason
spring	street	surround	terror	tight	treasure
spy	stretch	survive	test	time	treat
square	strike	suspect	than	tin	treaty
stage	string	suspend	thank	tiny	tree
stairs	strong	swallow	that	tire	trial
stamp	structure	swear	the	title	tribe
stand	struggle	sweet	theater	to	trick
star	study	swim	their	today	trip
start	stupid	symbol	theirs	together	troop
starve	subject	sympathy	them	tomorrow	trouble
state	substance	system	then	tone	truck
station	substitute	table	theory	tongue	true
status	succeed	tail	there	tonight	trust
stay	such	take	these	too	try

tube	**ve**getable	want	**wel**come	wild	word
turn	**ve**hicle	war	well	will	work
twice	**ver**sion	warm	west	win	world
tire	**ver**y	warn	wet	wind	**wor**ry
under	**ve**to	wash	what	**wind**ow	worse
under**stand**	**vi**cious	waste	wheat	wine	worth
unit	**vic**tim	watch	wheel	**win**g	wound
universe	**vic**tory	**wa**ter	when	**win**ter	wreck
un**less**	view	wave	where	wire	write
un**til**	**vio**lence	way	**whe**ther	wise	wrong
up	**vis**it	we	which	wish	yard
u**pon**	voice	weak	while	with	year
urge	**vol**ume	wealth	white	**with**draw	**yel**low
us	vote	**weap**on	who	with**out**	yes
use	wage	wear	whole	**wo**man	**yes**terday
valley	wait	**wea**ther	why	**won**der	yet
value	walk	week	wide	wood	you
vary	wall	weight	wife	wool	young

* (means that same word is used for a verb and a noun, with different stress)

When you learn a Globish word, you will not need to learn spelling rules or pronunciation rules. You will need to think of only that word. You should learn its individual pronunciation and how its individual spelling looks to you.

If you attempt to *sound out* every word from the English *spelling* **you will be sorry**. English writing has a very loose relationship with its sounds. But please...you must do everything to learn the **stressed** syllables in the Globish words.

102

If you will say that stressed syllable in a **heavy** tone, most people can understand the rest.

One key sound that *is* more important to Globish – and English – than any other is the *"schwa"* sound. The *schwa* is almost not a sound. It usually "fills in" in words of more than one syllable, as a way of moving quickly over unstressed syllables. The *schwa* also makes trying to spell using sound very difficult. Here are some examples of Globish- and English words that use the *schwa* and the letters that sound exactly the same when you say them:

i as in **penci**l, d**i**smiss, cris**i**s, **ferti**le

io as in **champ**io**n, **quest**io**n, **vers**io**n,

ie as in **pat**ie**nt

ia as in **parl**ia**ment, civil**ia**n, **spec**ia**l

au as in **au**thority

e as in **tak**e**n, **und**e**r, **syst**e**m

u as in **meas**u**re, **pict**u**re

ou as in **fam**ou**s,

iou as in **vic**iou**s, **ser**iou**s

ei as in **for**ei**gn

a as in **a**bove, **neutr**a**l

as in **purp_o_se, may_o_r, butt_o_n**

_ai_ as in **cert_ai_n**

_ua_ as in **us_ua_l**

All of these letters and letter-combinations will sound the same when an English speaker or a good Globish speaker says them. Using the _schwa_ on the unstressed syllable is the most important thing about Globish (or English) pronunciation – and spelling – that you can know, because it makes everything else so much easier.

Chapter 17
1500 Basic Globish Words Father 5000

The 1500 Globish words are useful in another way. They provide the basis for making many other words with slightly different meanings. We do that by four methods:

- Putting words together

- Adding a few letters to the front, or the back of a word. We call the basic words: "fathers" and the new words: "children."

- Using the same word for different Parts of Speech

- Using a **preposition** with verbs to make **Phrasal Verbs**

Putting two words together is fairly easy

The first word is really just an **adjective** for the last word. In the word *workman*, we can just say "What kind of man? A *workman* ." If the words are only one syllable, you stress the first syllable. Here are some of those *combined words*:

work	+	man	=	workman
bed	+	room	=	bedroom
class	+	room	=	classroom
day	+	time	=	daytime
week	+	end	=	weekend
home	+	work	=	homework
man	+	kind	=	mankind
air	+	plane	=	airplane
street	+	car	=	streetcar

Adding a few letters to the front or the back of a word

All of them are called *Affixes*. There are two basic kinds of *affixes*. The ones on the front of the word called *Prefixes*. The ones on the end of the words are called *Suffixes*.

Prefixes

Keep the original part of speech of the word that changes. Often, it changes the meaning a lot:

im + possible = impossible (not possible) adjective

in + correct = incorrect (not correct) adjective

un + happy = unhappy (not happy) adjective

re + new = renew (make new again) verb

re + turn = return (come back) verb

pre + view = preview (before the view) noun

Suffixes

Often the suffix changes the word slightly and usually changes the part of speech. Some of these words have already been made from prefixes.

possible + - ity = possibility adjective to noun

happy + -ness = happiness adjective to noun

renew + -al = renewal verb to noun

return + -able = returnable verb to adjective

special + - ly = specially adjective to adverb

The meanings of **affixes** may become very clear when you see that process happen a few times. **Care** + **less** means "with less care". **Care** + **ful** is "full of care."

Many times the same word can be used as a noun, a verb, and an adjective

Most of these words keep the same pronunciation when they change parts of speech. A **truck** (noun) is a way that farmers **truck** (verb) their corn to market. On the way they stop for coffee at a **truck** (adjective) stop. There are hundreds of these words in the Globish 1500. For instance, everyone has an **age**

A "truck" will "truck" its load... until the truck driver stops for coffee at a "truck stop."

(noun) and bad memory may be an **age** (adjective) **problem.** Also, we **age** (verb) good cheese.

Finally, some words are spelled the same, but change their syllable stress when they are used as a verb or noun. For example if it is a noun we say "**PRE**sent." But if it is a verb we say "to pre**SENT**." The same with the noun **RE**cord and the verb re**CORD**. However, there are only a few of these words in Globish.

Phrasal Verbs are made with simple verbs and prepositions... in a "verb phrase"

```
     Put              Take             Get
  Off /Up\ Out     Off /Up\ Out     Off /Up\ Out
  Down   Over      Down   Over      Down   Over
```

Phrasal verbs are so common that you cannot avoid them in Globish. We use many – like "**take out**" or"**put on**" or "**get up**" – hundreds of times daily. Even native English speakers forget that Phrasal Verbs are a verb phrase. Among these native speakers, new Phrasal Verbs are often created in less than a second. Some one will say we are going to "**Globish up**" our speech, which would mean we use all Globish words. Phrasal Verbs cause a huge amount of difficulty to some learners because they don't seem to make any sense. Even the best English teachers

Technical words

Preposition - a part of speech giving time or place relations to a noun.

Phrasal - made with a phrase, a group of words working together.

Adjective - a word which adds to or changes a noun

Affix - a group of new letters attached to the front or back of a word

Prefix - letters put on the front of a word, making it a different word.

Suffix - letters put on the front of a word, making it a different word

Adverb - a word which adds to or changes a verb, or an adjective disagree on understandable rules for Phrasal Verbs.

However, studies show that until age 10, English-speaking children use Phrasal Verbs and very little else. Globish should not miss that opportunity, because these verbs are among the most-used in English. Perhaps the best approach is for Globish user to simply "collect up" Phrasal Verbs that they see 2 or 3 times. They will be extremely useful. In many cases, the Phrasal Verb is the way that **both** native-English speakers and Globish speakers often avoid using a less common English verb.

Chapter 18
Cooking with Words

In this chapter – and much of this book – we describe elements that make up Globish. For those who have used some English, this will allow you to compare grammar in a little more detail. *But* it is NOT meant to teach Globish. We only want to inform future Globish users of its similarities using simple English grammar. So we hope this chapter is enough for readers to learn "about" Globish, though not enough to "learn" Globish.

S + V + O

Globish uses simple grammar, but following its grammar rules are very important. It is like putting a meal together with the words you have. It gives them an order that arrives at a good result. Most basic English learning now uses this kind of letter-notation to show the order of words in a sentence:

S = Subject - person or thing <u>making</u> the action

V = Verb - the action

O = Object - person or thing that <u>receives</u> the action

The first thing we observe is the general Voice or Mood of a sentence:

Active voice

Almost all of Globish will be in the Active Voice. In Globish, as in English, the main structure of the Active Voice is SUBJECT FIRST:

SUBJECT (person the sentence is about) + VERB (the action of the Subject).

> *I work on Sundays. I (S) work (V) on Sundays. (S + V)*

Many times this exact order also includes an OBJECT (noun or pronoun that the action is performed on).

> **I** *(S)* **know** *(V)* **Globish** *(Object)*. *(S + V + O)*

Sometimes there is an Indirect Object as well as a Direct Object.

> **I** *(S)* **give** *(V)* **you** *(IO)* **a present** *(DO)*. *(S + V + IO + DO)*

We add DO and NOT to the basic sentence to make it negative.

> **I** *(S)* **don't know** *(DO NOT + V)* **Spanish** *(O)*. *(S + DO NOT + V + O)*

We add the word *do* or *does* to begin a Question Sentence.

Do *(DO/DOES)* *you* *(S)* *know* *(V)* *French* *(O)?*
(DO/DOES + S + V + O?)

Another kind of Question begins with a Wh word. (Why, which, what, where, who, when)

When *(Wh)* *do* *(DO/DOES)* *you* *(S)* *drive* *(V)* *the car* *(O)?*

"THERE IS/THERE ARE" is the only kind of direct, Active voice statement where the subject comes after the verb. We use these for stating the existence of something.

There are *(V)* *two doctors* *(S)* *in town.*

Passive voice

Globish suggests that we *do not* use the Passive Voice very often. But sometimes it will be heard by students. Therefore you should know that it leaves the subject until the end, as in the previous sentence - *But sometimes it will be heard by students.* **But sometimes it will be heard by students** is a sentence we just used which is in Passive Voice. This means the Passive Voice requires (BE + V3) the third form of the verb, called the past participle. We might say *The program will be dropped completely.* ....**The program will be dropped** (V3) **completely**... You see there appears to be NO **S!** But *someone* dropped it.

113

That *someone* is the real subject, but the Passive Voice may leave it out.

Imperative mood (Demanding)

Do not walk on the grass. Drink 8 glasses of water every day. These sentences leave off the subject **You.** (You) **Do not walk on the grass.** (You) **Drink 8 glasses of water every day.** These are used if there is danger, or something is very important for other reasons. Again, we have left out the subject: **You,** in this case.

Conditional (About "If" and "Maybe")

Some people call it a Mood, others call it a Voice. It is very much like the Active Voice except that it uses Conditional words to change the meaning of the sentence.

1. **If I** (S) **move** (V) **to Spain, then I** (S) **will not speak** (WILL + NOT + V) **their language.**

2. **I** (S) **study** (V) **French** (O) **now**. BUT: **I** (S) **<u>might</u>** (MAY/MIGHT) **study** (V) **Italian** (O) **soon.**

Verbs and time

All Verbs are concerned in some way with the TIME the action happens.

I (S) **am** (V) **happy.** (means right NOW)

I (S) **was** (V) **happy**. (means BEFORE, NOT now.)

I (S) **will be** (V) **happy**. (means in FUTURE.)

Verb tenses

Tense means "time." **Verb Tenses** tell you the *relative time* the action took place. Globish may use as few as 6 - and up to 10 - of 12 verb tenses in English.

Present Simple	*I talk.* (S + V1)
Present Continuous	*I am talking.* (S + AM/ARE + V1 + ING)
Past Simple	*I talked.* (S + V2)
Past Continuous	*I was talking.* (S + WAS/WERE + V1 + ING)
Future Simple	*I will talk.* (S + WILL + V1)
Future Continuous	*I will be talking.* (S + WILL + BE + V1 + ING)
Present Perfect	*I have talked.* (S + HAVE + V3)
Present Perfect Continuous	*I have been talking.* (S + HAVE + BEEN + V1 + ING)
Past Perfect	*I had talked with him before last Tuesday.* (S + HAD + V3)
Future Perfect	*I will have talked with him by Monday (S + WILL + HAVE + V3)*

11 Past Perfect Continuous	(not in Globish) *He had been talking.*
12 Future Perfect Continuous	(not in Globish) *He will have been talking.*

As in the above chart, all verbs have 3 forms. Some samples:

(V1) **talk** (V2) **talked** (V3) **talked**

(V1) **let** (V2) **let** (V3) **let**

(VI) **go** (V2) **went** (V3) **gone**

When the verb tense is easily changed with an ending, we call it "regular." However, there are about 100 "irregular" verbs in Globish which have different patterns or different words to make the 3 tenses.

Verbs as Nouns

Many times verbs are used as nouns. Then

Technical words

Pronoun - a substitute for a noun: "man" becomes "he."

Negative - what something is NOT. "Mary is **not** happy."

Participle - the third form of a verb: 1. go 2. went 3. gone

Imperative - a sentence which **demands** you do something.

Conditional - a verb form which says something **could** happen.

Articles - **a, an**, or **the**. these tells you if a noun is any of the same things, or if we are talking about just one.

Infinitive - uses the basic verb form with "to" in order to make a noun phrase. "Children like to play."

International words

Phones - devices for talking and texting over long distances.

Data – The information in computers and cell phones

they are not really a verb in the sentence, but a "thing."

Swimming (S) **is** (V) **fun.**

I (S) **like** (V) **swimming** (O).

Also many times the infinitive form of the verb becomes a noun object. Again, they are like nouns and are not acting as action verbs.

I (S) **like** (V) **to swim** (O).

On Articles

Some languages like English have articles *a, an* and *the* to show if any noun is general or is the only one. *A* teacher could be *any* teacher. *The* teacher is the one for *this class only*.

On Learning Globish

There are several methods to learn Globish now, and more are being created. First, many English teachers have made their own Globish courses. They used the first books in French by Jean Paul Nerrière *Don't Speak English - Parlez Globish* and *Découvrez le Globish (*with Jacques Bourgon and Phillipe Dufresne*).*

On the Internet at *jpn-globish. com (French)*, *Globish. com* and *bizeng. net* are sources now. New teacher-created courses continue to happen the world over from Korea to Hungary to India and back.

An Internet online course called Globish IN Globish™ (GNG) is offered by David Hon. The same lessons operate "cross-platform" on *both* computers and cell phones – with low bandwidth pages data costs. The new GNG will allow any English learner who can read 350 words to start learning everything using *only* Globish. That person learns 44 more of the most-used Globish words in every lesson, to the full 1500. At the same time, GNG offers simple, correct, grammar and sentence structure, as well as listening and pronunciation practice.

In addition to providing this book, and GNG, in the near future, Globish.com will offer several directions for beginners learning Globish in their own languages. Many of these courses will be on the Internet and in other materials packaged for easy use by the student and instructor. The first of these courses will be in Spanish and Hindi, but others are being designed for specific global business needs.

Chapter 19
Say "No" to Most Figurative Language

One of the extremely useful rules in Globish is about *figurative language*. This is one area which is extremely difficult for English speakers when they use Globish. If we use this rule completely, we might think Globish would not be any fun. (However, it is almost impossible for people not to smile when they like each other.) There are three areas Globish observes very carefully:

Idioms such as *"crash and burn"* (make a major mistake) or *"miss the boat"* (do something too late) are often difficult in learning **any** new language, for several reasons: They vary greatly between every language and even in the same language. For instance, British men who are visiting the homes of female friends *"knock them up"* as in knocking on the door. However, in the American idiom *"knock up"* means **to make a woman pregnant**. At times, laughter results from that usage between the two cultures. The person using Globish is understandably confused. In addition, **idioms move in and out of popularity** in social classes, professions, and different age groups. Say an American young person is told to "shake a leg" – (to *hurry*). He knows an old person is talking because the idiom was popular in the 1950's.

Analogies are often used in many languages to communicate new ideas simply. Much of the time, however, they are difficult to translate into other cultures. We may say that an idea is *as old as last week's newspaper*. What if someone only had a newspaper once every week? Or sees one newspaper every year? Some **analogies** can be used IF the speaker or writer is CERTAIN that they will be taken the same way they are offered. (Note that we tried a few in this book.)

Negative Questions Asking for Positive Response. Often English speakers ask: *Is it not time for a coffee break?* (You will get silence, but no coffee.) Because of these difficulties, it is always a good idea to answer with more than *Yes* or *No*. Saying *Yes, it is* or *No it isn't* will resolve a lot of confusions.

Humor may happen if two people see something they both think is funny. It may be a small baby reaching up for whatever she can pull down. Or a monkey walking strangely like a man. People do enjoy each other through shared humor. However, the attempt to create and communicate humor in a new language is *dangerous*. These things make that kind of "language humor" **NOT advisable** in Globish because:

Possibly the humor won't be understood

That's the best worst case. Even people who speak variations of English may not understand each others' jokes.

Some people, at some points, will just not "get it"

Even within the same culture, some people may have their mind on something else. Other kinds of people just take statements more *exactly* than others intend. *"I'm going to rope in some friends to help me"* may seem like harmless humor. But some people will go looking around for the rope. All of these factors are far more probable in non-native speakers.

Different people think different things are funny

A holy man, for example, may not think jokes about the church are funny. Jokes about body parts seem funny to teen-aged boys, but they don't tell their mothers.

It can cause high insult to another's

Technical words

Knock - hit with the hard part of your hand, as on a door

Metaphor - word in place of another: "Swimming in money"

Personifications - using a person's name to suggest qualities.

Antithetical - the opposite of what something seems to mean.

system of beliefs.

Created humor often relies on one or another element of figurative language, which makes its funny meanings difficult to communicate. Also, most humor is usually at someone else's expense. It usually means we are looking down on someone else. For example, it is very possible that – in the near future – non-native speakers will have many new jokes about native English speakers.

Chapter 20
Globish "Best Practices"

"Responsible" communication in Globish

A lot of people who use Globish have gotten some English already, in many ways. So it is not good to make too many rules, but rather to show Best Practices. *Best Practices* in computers, for instance, help us use programs in the greatest number of different machines. One clear area in Globish is with clauses and phrases.

Globish supports correct English in any sentence, but long clauses and phrases can cause many problems. These can even be difficult even for average English speakers. Try not to use too many modifying or reflexive clauses like: *I do not trust a man who shakes his stick at a friendly dog.* Or: *We do not know where the keys to the back door were hidden.* **Better in Globish**: *I do not trust that man. He shakes his stick at a friendly dog.* Or: *We cannot find the keys to the back door. They are hidden somewhere.*

Even more difficult, of course, are clauses which may need the words such as *that* or *whom.* The native English speaker leaves out those key words about 50% of the time. For him or her, that word is known and expected to exist, but is left silent. Therefore a non-native speaker hears: *He's the man I sold the house to.* And yet something is missing. In the most-correct English that should be: *He's the man to whom I sold the house.* And even in common English it would be: *He's the man who I sold the house to.* **Better in Globish:** *I sold the house to that man.* Or, *"See that person? I sold the house to him."*

Perhaps the most often left-out word in these clauses is *that.* *"There are many reasons the government cannot reduce your taxes"* is, of course, missing the word *"that."* Often the Globish speaker depends on hearing the word *that.* He or she knows *a clause is coming* which will have its own subject and verb. The native speaker of English thinks nothing of leaving out the word *that.* But the beginning speaker may be lost. **Better in Globish**: Always use the word *that.* **Best in Globish:** Remake the sentence (s) to say: *The government cannot reduce your taxes. Of course, there are many reasons.* So, English speakers should always use the words *that* or *who* in **modifying** clauses or phrases they say to Globish speakers. And often, with a little thought, they can make those longer sentences into shorter ones that work as well or better.

Punctuation

In writing, there are several punctuation tricks that will really make the writing easier for the Globish person to understand. These can be used more than the English speaker will use them, because there is more need for clear understanding in a new language. You can use **dashes** (–) to separate an extra set of thoughts – like we do here – and that can be very helpful. Also **ellipses** (…) will show a stop in the thought, or make other kinds of separations in ideas such as including words which *should* be there. Most computers will allow easy use of **bold**, *italics*, or <u>underlining</u> make certain parts of a sentence more clear. *Globish speakers should use these "punctuation tricks" at* **any** *time it makes their written communication easier to understand.*

Sentence Fragments

Many English teachers who teach formal English want students to write complete thoughts, and tell them *"Never start a sentence with "And" or "But."* But for Globish, it is the other way. And starting with "But" helps it to be a shorter sentence, an easier thought to understand. Or "and". (Or "or"...:) So the Globish speaker should look instead to the many writers who write for periodicals and newspapers.

Numbers

Some words for the lesser numbers – like *one* and *two* – may be spelled out in Globish. The method of just using the number itself should be acceptable to all in Globish. Larger numbers have some cultural differences. For instance, America uses 1,500 for the number of words in the Globish vocabulary. Europe uses 1'500, or 1.500, or 1 500. *No one is correct!* So it would seem that the common sense way is to leave the number as 1500. With very large numbers like $1 million and 1 billion people, these international words help to avoid counting zeroes (0).

Technical words

Reflexive - a grammar word for words **that** "go back" to a subject or object. "The man **who** came to dinner."

Modify - changes or adds to. Adjectives **modify** nouns.

Assume - thinking that something exists, or is true.

Punctuation - marks that show things about words or sentences.

Dashes - punctuation marks that show extra thoughts in sentences.

Ellipses - ... Marks used too end a thought softly, or insert a word.

Bold - makes a word or words darker than the words around.

Italics - makes a word or words more angled than words around.

Fragments - a part cut from the whole. "Sentence Fragments" are not whole sentences. (But sometimes they work OK.)

Chapter 21
Critical Sounds for Global Understanding

In the past, various English teaching systems have put forth their versions of a standard English pronunciation. They usually demand that students from many mother tongues learn many sounds that are unusual to them. Differences between English, American, and other dialects make it much more difficult. And then the task becomes *even* more difficult when students attempt to match those many new sounds to English spelling.

The generally-accepted fact that non-English speakers can understand each other's Globish opens up an interesting possibility. It seems possible that some sounds from one's mother tongue, even if not perfect, can be "enough" for understanding. Language experts of the last century provided very complete collections of sounds from mother tongues that were not present in English. Yet in many cases, students could easily provide substitute sounds from their own mother tongues that could be understood. The main problem for native English speakers seems to be the "accent" of non-native speakers. (Other very strong "accents" from different parts of London, and between America and other former colonies, seem less problematic.)

A study this year in comparative linguistics had English students from 6 mother-tongues recording the same list of words, and a reading of the same story. These were middle-to-high-level students of English who had spent a short period of time in an English-speaking country. The students were from Mainland China, France, Poland, India, Hungary, and Germany. All of these students could understand each other well in what we would call Globish-level words and grammar.

Then a native English speaker was brought in (in this case an American) who had not met any of them or lived in any of their countries. He listened to each recording and wrote down only what he could understand. The study was made over a 3-month period with 2 weeks between each listening activity for the native speaker.

The study had interesting outcomes and perhaps even more interesting possibilities. Because we think the possibilities are worthy of note, we should observe more closely what materials were used. All 6 students recorded the following list of words:

sounds	the given words	sounds	the given words	sounds	the given words	sounds	the given words
ɒ	lot	ʃ	ship	ɪə	here	u	situation
ɒ	wash	ʃ	sure	ɪə	near	u	you
ɑˑ	father	ə	about	j	few	ʊ	foot
ɑˑ	start	ə	common	j	yet	ʊ	put
æ	bad	ɜˑ	learn	k	key	uː	blue
æ	trap	ɜˑ	nurse	k	school	uː	group
aɪ	high	eə	fair	l	feel	ʊə	cure
aɪ	try	eə	various	l	light	ʊə	poor
aʊ	mouth	eɪ	break	m	sum	v	move
aʊ	now	eɪ	face	m	move	v	view
b	black	əʊ	no	n	nice	ʌ	blood
b	job	əʊ	show	n	sun	ʌ	mud
ɔˑ	law	f	coffee	ŋ	ring	w	queen
ɔˑ	war	f	fat	ŋ	sung	w	was
ɔɪ	boy	g	get	p	copy	z	buzz
ɔɪ	choice	g	ghost	p	pen	z	zero
d	dream	h	hand	r	during	ʒ	pleasure
d	odd	h	hot	r	right	ʒ	vision
ð	smooth	ɪ	bid	s	music	θ	path
ð	this	ɪ	kid	s	soon	θ	thing
dʒ	age	i	glorious	t	button		
dʒ	soldier	i	happy	t	tea		
e	bed	iː	fleece	tʃ	church		
e	dress	iː	sea	tʃ	match		

And all 6 students also recorded themselves reading this story:

It all happened at about 6 p.m. on a Sunday evening. The soldier went into the church. He was dressed in a uniform and one could see blood on it. It wasn't just his vision, it was a lot more. And it wasn't his choice. He tried to put the ring next to his other things but his hands didn't move. He didn't feel well. He was in a trap and he knew it.. "The key to the vault" he thought. "I should start it right now". He wanted his poor wife, who was a nurse, and his kids to get all his belongings, before he... But the situation was absolutely different. But just then his face went black and he wasn't sure if it was just his dream. He could see the blue sea and hear some soft music. Soon he had a nice view as well: everyone looked happy now and sipped tea or coffee. "But what does it show?" he had various thoughts. "Aren't they just ghosts here?" But he had no more thoughts ever. There was a war out there…

From this small study, it appears that there are only 7 sounds that are still a problem for all of the students. The sounds which were a problem for everyone were the vowels in the words: **mud** (*mUd*) **near** (*nEAr*) **no** (*nO*) **now** (*nOW*) *face* (*fAce*) **bad** (*bAd*) and the soft "th" consonant in *thing (THing)*.

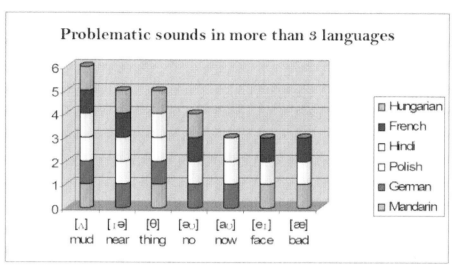

Problematic sounds in more than 3 languages

However, other findings of the study were equally interesting. We can also observe which sounds are most difficult in individual mother tongues, and with that knowledge, make the number of required sounds even more exact.

Sound Production Difficulties from the Different Mother Tongues

It appears that these individuals from each mother tongue also had trouble – when they spoke English – with an extra, adapted set of sounds. These sounds were: (1) *not in their native tongue* **and** (2) gave them a *few* more difficult sounds to produce. These sounds – *not* in the native tongues and causing a few extra problems for each student – are in bold, italic letters in the tables below:

Sounds	Sounds the Polish speaker had difficulties with									
Sounds	æ	θ	ʌ	aʊ	ɪə	i:	tʃ	h	ɒ	ŋ
Words	bad	thing	mud	now	near	sea	match	hand	lot	ring

Sounds	Sounds the Mandarin speaker had difficulties with									
Sounds	d	dʒ	æ	v	θ	ð	eə	eɪ	ʊə	ʌ
Words	dream	age	bad	move	thing	this	fair	face	cure	mud

Sounds	Sounds the Hindi speaker had difficulties with									
Sounds	θ	ð	eɪ	ʌ	əʊ	ɔɪ	aʊ	ɪə	ʒ	aɪ
Words	thing	this	face	mud	no	boy	now	near	vision	try

Sounds	Sounds the Hungarian speaker had difficulties with						
Sounds	θ	eə	ʊə	ʌ	əʊ	ɪə	w
Words	thing	fair	cure	mud	no	near	was

Sounds	Sounds the French speaker had difficulties with					
Sounds	æ	eɪ	ʌ	əʊ	ɪə	ɑ⃞
Words	bad	face	mud	no	near	start

	Sounds the German speaker had difficulties with					
Sounds	θ	ʌ	əʊ	ɔɪ	aʊ	ɪə
Words	thing	mud	no	boy	now	near

There may not be as many extra difficulties here as we thought there would be. At the most, the Mandarin speaker has 6 other sounds that are difficult to understand. The fewest extra sounds came from the French and German speakers. We might suspect these results happen because both languages are closer in roots to English. Of course, there are many reasons that this was not a complete study. However, as it stands right now, this study presents a reasonable set of ideas on which to base some early – but useful – decisions:

1. *Most* mother tongues already contain *most* of the sounds that are necessary for understanding between people who speak Globish.

2. These sounds should also be largely understandable by native English speakers.

3. There are – at most – 8 to 13 sounds that are missing in any given mother tongue – for understandable Globish pronunciation. So Globish speakers must learn to produce those few sounds *understandably* for the times that they are necessary. All the **rest** of the accepted English sounds would

apply only to those students who wish to speak English with little or no accent at all.

4. Only one of the sounds which were difficult for all was a **consonant**: the "th" sound in _thing_, _thick_ and _both_. The other six were **vowel** sounds.

5. For Globish, it may be possible that **understandable vowel** sounds - often brought from the native tongue – are necessary _only_ on the stressed syllable.

6. The finding in #5, plus an expected placement of the words within simple grammar, could limit the range of sounds necessary for Globish talking. If the listener doesn't hear words in the order he or she expects, he will be more likely to think the pronunciation is wrong. This is why the native listener clearly understood the students' pronunciation much better within the story recordings.

7. Mastering the sounds and the stresses with only 1500 words is rewarding in two ways:

- There is not a need for the many rules tying spelling and pronunciation which is such a large problem for English students.

- Many native English speakers will admit that they remember spelling only partly by sound association, and the other part is visual memory. So learning both the sound and *the image* of a word may be the most effective way of learning the 1500 Globish words.

8. It would follow from this study that each student from each mother tongue would have a slightly different path to Globish. However, it is likely that most of the sound production problems will happen in the student's first 350 words. This is a time when almost any language looks impossible to the student.

9. The syllable-stress problems will clearly happen more when students are faced with longer words and more varied stress. However, the problem grows if the student did not learn the few new vowel sounds that are truly necessary to use on the stressed syllables.

10. Thus, if these early findings are even partly correct, then there are probably only a few *new* Globish

> **Technical words**
>
> Consonants - the letter sounds around the vowels.
>
> Vowels - in English and Globish - A, E, I, O, and U with variation.

sounds that are not in students' native languages. Clearly, Globish speakers will need to produce these few sounds well – from the start. But this important rule would allow Globish students to have clear goals from the beginning, and clear measurements at the end of their Globish study.

It is "enough" to understand, and to be understood.

Chapter 22
Globish in Texting?

hi jack, check ur mails. i hv
sent smth to u. just got a mail
from italy. remember? Stephano!
d guy who spent 2 yrs here in
d states. gr8 news. blv me! ull
luv it...ttyl

Millions and millions of people of every culture and nationality are now communicating on the Internet and on the face of their mobile phones. Much of the time, people with different mother tongues are *texting*, using "a little" English that they learned in school. It's not perfect English. But these may be the people who can easily learn Globish: The texting words that people are using almost never fall outside of the Globish 1500. The sentences are active and with simple construction. And the shortening of words means that everyone knows the sounds that are left out. (In fact, many writing systems in the world leave out the vowels, assuming speakers of the language would know those sounds. Basically,

English – and Globish – do the same with the schwa sounds, with letters which look nothing like that sound on the unstressed syllable.) But to be understandable, *the English must be very correct in form* – almost a model for Globish. The goal is not to have the other person love your English words or skills, but only to communicate. Perhaps that is why the word "Globish" seems to come up anywhere on the Internet where people of different native tongues are communicating with each other.

Some people will say this communication would match any kind of simple English needed between people who have learned "enough" to use it across cultures. That would be a good explanation except (1) when talking about skill levels, they often say they use "Globish" instead of "English;" (2) a high number of the references to Globish are in Blogs, forums, chat rooms, and other places that can be searched. These people seem to be seeking a simple structure they can depend on. And a new name for it.

> *hi joe, r u talking abt d guy w d american girlfrn? yeap, i no him. i thought he hd gone bk to italy. i don't hv time rght now to check my mails but will. hv to go now. Cu*

(Above: Hi Joe. Are you talking about the guy with the American girlfriend? Yes, I know him. I though he had gone

back to Italy. I don't have time right now to check my mails but will…Have to go now. See You.)

Note that the sounds in "r" "u" "no" (for "know") and "CU" (See you) are important for understanding. In many cases, the amount of usage of a word allows it to be shortened, as in "abt", "d" (for "the"), "w" ("with") "girlfrn", "hd", "bk", "rght" are all common Globish and English words, so most people know them when they are shortened. The small "i" is a universal sign of the worldwide Internet. No one is important enough to be "I."

Texting is very like the old "shorthand" used by Secretaries to take dictation (before voice recorders), for their bosses' letters, or at important meetings. Shorthand is still used in a very few cases, when meeting members have to remember points in detail and do not want their voices recorded. With shorthand, Secretaries shorten everything, so the words and phrases can be spelled out in full at a later time. There were basically two types of shorthand: (1) that which only the writer could understand at a later time and (2) that which *any* other person who knew those shorthand forms could read exactly. Pittman's, for example, is shorthand that other people can also read, and it was quite important in British business prior to computers.

hi jack, y r u so busy? r u still working? im sorry. once u hv read d mail ull forget all of ur probs...its btr than anything else. and yes, u r rght. stephano hs gone bk to italy. any guess?

One thing is clear from the texting we see in millions of chats, quick messages, and mobile phone messaging: everyone is now becoming a shorthand expert. It is easier to learn and use this kind of texting "shorthand" when everyone knows it will be at broadly-understood level. If you have a) a small number of most-used words, like the Globish 1500, and b) simple grammatical forms, you can easily use **texting**. The limitations of Globish can easily fit **texting** as it is happening now.

hi joe, OMG! i cnt blv this. u r rght. thats gr8! so stephano hs invited us to go to italy this summer! cool. and it means we cd visit many oder countries and all of our frnds over there. im so excited. lets meet and talk abt it asap.

But are people just "**lazy**", **texting** when they should write out whole words? Not really....

Time and Space

Most of the important discoveries are somehow about Time and Space. When people are "chatting" online, or using instant messaging between computers or mobile phones, they demand *speed* of answering back. Why? Because "chat" is real-time, like being on the phone, and young people don't want to appear stupid because they seem slow to answer. Picture two girls in the back corners of a school classroom, texting on their mobiles to friends in other classes. Watch their eyes roll if some friend is slow to answer back. It is a talk – like a face-to-face talk – and the more it "moves" like a real talk between people, the quicker the response that is *expected*. That is why many answers back are simply "K", or "CU" or "CIAO".

There are also tools to help with the items that you would usually have in talking face-to-face. If you want something to be funny, people can usually tell by the smile on your face. That is why the "emoticons" like …☺ and …☹ now appear from most texting when the symbols …:) and …:(are put in. And most Internet users know (LOL) for "Laughing Out Loud." Means that you are sharing something you think is funny. If some people didn't see (LOL) they won't know what you said was meant to be funny. Also these tools help give a quick response, and that is part of Timing. Or Time…

> *hi jack, u see? lets meet 2nite. we dnt hv time to waste. lets make a gr8 plan and get bk w it to stephano so he cn prepare eg. i cd b at ur place by 7.*

Space Means Cost

As for space, there are severe data limitations on some mobile phone texting. Some of us remember old films where news comes of events far away via a telegram. People were charged by the *word* then. Their messages were much like what you might see on a mobile phone now. "Home 7 pm train Friday. Miss you. George."

Just the viewing size on some **mobile phones**, and the difficulty of entering **text**, makes people use the shortened words and sentences. In much of the world...160 characters are allowed for 1 message costing say $ .25 (US). If the message is even 161 characters, you have to pay another $ .25 for another message!

Even within the same culture, people do not seem to use any more English than the common Globish words in the **mobile phone** texting. **Space = Cost...**

COST! COST! COST!

In much of the world...160 characters are allowed for 1 message costing about 25 cents. If the message is even 161 characters, you have to pay for another message! Good *Texting* makes them short...and understood.

If you can read this book and and can use even 1000 of the most-used Globish words, then maybe you have also been **texting** on computer **chats** and on **mobile phones** for years.

> *hi jack, i hv ordered pizza 4 2nite. we r gonna fix eg and hv a gr8 time in italy. till then ciao*

But you won't find recent books to study on Globish texting. Instead, you will live it, on your mobile phones and on the Internet. And perhaps most of all, u wll hv fun... ☺

Technical words

Texting - writing on the Internet or Mobil Phone, in chats, emails.

Blog - B-Log: where one person writes ideas on a regular basis.

Chat - talk in seconds using texting on the Internet.

Forums - where many people can put in their thoughts.

International words

Mobile Phone - also called "cell phone." Used more than TVs.

Screen - the surface on devices where you watch pictures or text

TV (Television) - the box with a picture that doesn't let you "chat" with it. (lol ...☺)

Chapter 23
When Globish Arrives

Since 2004, when the first books about Globish were published, the talk about Globish has changed. In that year, in forums on the Internet, many English teachers looked at the idea – and then looked away, saying: "I cannot imagine anything important being said in Globish" and "They are going to destroy our beautiful English language" and "Why can't they just learn how to speak decent English?" These forums are still on the Internet. You can Google them.

But many more people were still traveling from their countries, and still joining global businesses. Many more in this period were leaving their countries on work-permits for the first time to take jobs in more prosperous countries. They could not wait, they had to speak and be heard. And because they were speaking English across the world, more people began to see what these people with just "enough" English could really do. They built roads and houses, but many also made scientific discoveries and many more made lots of money in new worldwide businesses. All of this with just "enough" English.

Now, 5 years later, the tone toward Globish has changed. Most people now accept that native English speakers will not rule the world. Most people accept that there are important leaders who speak only "enough" English, but use it well to lead very well in the world.

So now there are very different questions, in the same forums. Some of the same people from 2004 are now asking:

"How many people now know enough English?".

"Should the native English-speaking teachers, who said 'you will never be good enough' now still be the guards over the language?" and

"Who will own the language?" And some few are beginning to ask: "How much English is enough?"

We think Globish – as described in this book – carries many of the answers.

Globish developed from observations and recording of what seemed to be the usual limitations of the average non-native speakers of English. Perhaps only 10% of those have studied English more than a year, or lived for a year in an English-speaking country. But they may have enough, if they know what *is* enough.

Perhaps in the next 5 years, more people will run out of money for never-ending English classes. And more people will decide to follow careers and have families and … live…instead of always trying – year after year – for that goal of perfect English.

Globish may have their answer. And it may also have the answer for global companies who need enough English – but perhaps not perfect English – in their home offices and sales branches. Globish might work for these companies if their native speakers will – at the same time – learn how much English is too much.

Globish is what Toronto University linguist Jack Chambers called in 2009 "a new thing and very interesting…if (they are) formally codifying it, then Globish will gain status."

This book has been written not only to describe and codify, but to demonstrate Globish as a natural language, yet one that is in a closed system that is predictable and dependable, and is very close to being used across the globe now.

Then with so many good reasons for Globish that so many people agree with, why hasn't it happened? Why hasn't it arrived?

There seem to be 3 main barriers to that arrival:

Physical: People think they do not have the time or the money or the nearness to English Speaking to learn enough as a tool.

With new media and Internet courses, this will make Globish all the easier to learn.

Language: Many English speakers truly feel that you cannot have just part of a language and you must always try for all of it. Quite a few language professors say that Globish is "not studied enough" or "not structured enough" – as always, without saying how much IS enough.

Political: The questions of who will make Globish happen, and who will require it, and who will finally "own" it seem central here. The remaining people who speak against Globish will discover that the citizens of the world will require it, make it happen, and own it – likely within the next 10 years. The very name *Globish* establishes this new point of view – that of the Global citizen who does not need the English past. This citizen needs only a dependable, usable language for the future.

Although it may not be historically exact, one has the image of the poor, beaten Englishmen who brought forth the Magna Carta in 1215. They were ruled by the foreign Normans, and the Normans wrote all the English laws in French, which the poor people in England could not understand. Along with others, these common people stood up before their Kings, at great risk to their families and themselves. And they said: "Enough!" They were frightened but still brave. Carrying only knives and clubs, they demanded that the laws by which they lived be more fair, and be given out in their own language – English.

Globish could be the interesting next step for the world…when people use English to be freed from the English. Globish will arrive when these common people from every country in the world, stand up and say "Enough." And Globish, as you see it here, will be there to give them…enough. When Globish arrives, you will talk to someone who just a few years ago could not understand you …and turned away. And you will write in Globish to someone who understands and answers – perhaps even with a job or a good school possibility…Then you will look at these few words of Globish and say…

> *"How rich I am…. Look at all of these words I have…So many words for so many opportunities and so many new friends…Look at all that I can do with them…. What valuable words they are…And I know them all!"*

Appendix

U.S. President Barack Obama's Inauguration Address

Below are side-by-side versions of President Barack Obama's Inauguration Address in Washington DC on January 20, 2009, which he delivered before a crowd of 2 million people. On the left is the exact version (with his non-Globish words in **black**). On the right is the way it might have sounded in Globish.

English Version

My fellow citizens:

*I stand here today **humbled** by the task before us, **grateful** for the trust you have **bestowed**, mindful of the sacrifices borne by our ancestors. I thank President Bush for his service to our nation, as well as the **generosity** and cooperation he has shown throughout this **transition**.*

Globish Version

My friends and citizens:

I stand here today full of respect for the work before us. I want to thank you for the trust you have given, and I remember all the things given up by the people who came before us. I thank President Bush for his service to our nation, as well as for the spirit of giving and cooperation he has shown during this change-over.

44 Americans have now taken the presidential **oath**. The words have been spoken during rising **tides** of **prosperity** and the still waters of peace. Yet, every so often the **oath** is taken amidst gathering clouds and **raging** storms. At these **moments**, America has carried on not simply because of the skill or vision of those in high office, but because We the People have remained faithful to the **ideals** of our **forbearers**, and true to our **founding** documents.

44 Americans have now been sworn in as president. The words have been spoken during rising waves of wealth and well-being and the still waters of peace. Yet, every so often, these words of honor are spoken surrounded by gathering clouds and wild storms. At these times, America has carried on not simply because those in high office were skilled or could see into the future. But it has been because We the People have kept believing in the values of our first fathers, and stayed true to the documents that created our country.

So it has been. So it must be with this **generation** of Americans.

So it has been. So it must be with this modern-day population of Americans.

*That we are in the midst of crisis is now well understood. Our nation is at war, against a far-reaching **network** of violence and hatred. Our economy is badly weakened, a **consequence** of **greed** and irresponsibility on the part of some, but also our collective failure to make hard choices and prepare the nation for a new age.*

It is well understood now that we are in the middle of a crisis. Our nation is at war, against a far-reaching, organized system of violence and hate. Our economy has been badly weakened. This is the result of extreme desire for great wealth by some people, and failure to act responsibly. But we have all failed to make hard choices and to get the nation ready for a new age.

*Homes have been lost; jobs shed; businesses **shuttered**. Our health care is too costly; our schools fail too many; and each day brings further evidence that the ways we use energy strengthen our **adversaries** and threaten our **planet**. These are the **indicators** of crisis, subject to **data** and **statistics**. Less measurable but no less*

Homes have been lost; jobs given up; businesses have closed. Our health care costs too much; our schools fail too many; and each day brings further proof that the ways we use energy make those against us stronger and threaten our world. These are the ways we can measure a crisis. Another problem is just *profound is a **sapping** of confidence across our land – a **nagging** fear that America's decline is **inevitable**, and that the next **generation** must lower its sights.*

*Today I say to you that the challenges we face are real. They are serious and they are many. They will not be met easily or in a short **span** of time. But know this, America – they will be met. On this day, we gather because we have chosen hope over fear, unity of purpose over **conflict** and **discord**.*

*On this day, we come to **proclaim** an end to the petty **grievances** and false promises, the **recriminations** and worn*

as great, but we cannot measure it as easily. It is the draining of our own belief in America – a fear that America's fall is surely coming and that future Americans must lower their hopes.

Today I say to you that the trials we face are real. They are serious and they are many. They will not be met easily or in a short time. But know this, America – they will be met. On this day we gather because we have chosen hope over fear. We have chosen united purpose over fighting and over noisy argument.

On this day we come to announce an end to narrow-minded arguing, to the lies, and to the accusing and worn *out dogmas, that for far too long have **strangled** our politics.*

*We remain a young nation, but in the words of **Scripture**, the time has come to set aside childish things. The time has come to **reaffirm** our **enduring** spirit; to choose our better history; to carry forward that **precious** gift, that **noble** idea, passed on from generation to generation: the God-given **promise** that all are equal, all are free, and all deserve a chance to **pursue** their full measure of happiness. In **reaffirming** the greatness of our nation, we understand that greatness is never a given. It must be earned. Our **journey** has never been one of short-cuts or settling for less. It has not been the path for the **faint-hearted** – for those who **prefer leisure** over work, or seek only the pleasures of riches and*

out teachings that for far too long have killed our politics.

We remain a young nation, but in the words of the Holy Book, the time has come to put away childish things. The time has come to back up again our timeless spirit; to choose our better history; to carry forward that valued gift. This is the honored idea that has passed on from father and mother to child. It is the God-given truth that we are all equal, all are free, and all should have a chance to seek their full measure of happiness. We are confirming and rebuilding the greatness of our nation. But we understand that greatness is never a given. It must be earned. Our history has never been one of short-cuts or settling for less. It has not *fame.*

*Rather, it has been the risk-takers, the doers, the makers of things – some celebrated but more often men and women **obscure** in their labor, who have carried us up the long, **rugged** path towards **prosperity** and freedom.*

For us, they packed up their few worldly possessions and traveled across oceans in search of a new life.

*For us, they **toiled** in **sweatshops** and settled the West; **endured** the **lash** of the **whip** and plowed the hard earth.*

been the path for the weak-hearted – for those who want to play instead of work, or to seek only the comfort of richness and popularity.

Instead, we should honor the risk-takers, the ones who "do," the makers of things. Some of them were celebrated but more often they were men and women hidden in their labor. They were the ones who carried us up the long, rough path toward freedom and the good life.

For us, they took their few material belongings and travelled across oceans in search of a new life.

For us, they worked long hours in low-paying factories and settled in the West. They were beaten by the slave-master's stick and worked the hard earth.

*For us, they fought and died, in places like Concord and Gettysburg; Normandy and Khe Sahn. Time and again these men and women struggled and **sacrificed** and worked till their hands were **raw** so that we might live a better life.*

*They saw America as bigger than the **sum** of our individual **ambitions**; greater than all the differences of birth or wealth or **faction**. This is the **journey** we continue today. We remain the most **prosperous**, powerful nation on Earth. Our workers are no less productive than when this crisis began. Our minds are no less inventive, our goods and services no less needed than they were last week or last month or last year.*

For us, they fought and died, in places like Concord and Gettysburg; Normandy and Khe San. Time and again these men and women struggled and sacrificed and worked till their hands were torn open so that we might have a better life.

They saw America as bigger than the total of our individual dreams added up together; greater than all the differences of birth, wealth or social group. This is a path that we continue to travel today. We remain the most successful, powerful nation on Earth. Our workers produce no less than when the crisis began. Our minds are no less able to invent, our goods and services no less

Our **capacity** *remains* **undiminished**. *But our time of standing* **pat**, *of protecting narrow interests and putting off unpleasant decisions – that time has surely passed. Starting today, we must pick ourselves up, dust ourselves off, and begin again the work of remaking America. For everywhere we look, there is work to be done. The state of the economy calls for action,* **bold** *and* **swift**, *and we will act - not only to create new jobs, but to lay a new* **foundation** *for growth. We will build the roads and bridges, the electric grids and digital lines that feed our* **commerce** *and* **bind** *us together. We will* **restore** *science to its rightful place, and wield technology's*

necessary than they were last week or last month or last year.

Our power has not decreased. But our time of standing down, of protecting selfish interests and putting off hard decisions – that time has surely passed. Starting today, we must pick ourselves up, dust ourselves off, and begin again the work of remaking America. For everywhere we look, there is work to be done. The condition of our economy calls for something to be done, brave and quick. And we will act - not only to create new jobs, but to create a new environment for growth. We will build the roads and bridges, the electric system and computer lines that feed the trade in our markets and connect us to *wonders to raise health care's quality and lower its cost. We will **harness** the sun and the winds and the soil to fuel our cars and run our factories. And we will **transform** our schools and colleges and universities to meet the demands of a new age. All this we can do. And all this we will do.*

*Now, there are some who question the scale of our **ambitions** - who suggest that our system cannot **tolerate** too many big plans. Their memories are short. For they have forgotten what this country has already done; what free men and women can achieve when imagination is joined to common purpose, and necessity to*

each other. We will return science to its right place, and use technology's wonders to raise health care's quality and lower its cost. We will capture the sun and the winds and the soil to fuel our cars and run our factories. And we will improve our schools and colleges and universities to meet the demands of a new age. All this we can do. And all this we will do.

Now there are some who question the scale of our plans – who suggest that our system cannot accept too many big plans. Their memories are short. For they have forgotten what this country has already done. They have forgotten what free men and women can achieve when imagination is *courage.*

*What the **cynics** fail to understand is that the ground has shifted beneath them – that the **stale** political arguments that have consumed us for so long no longer apply. The question we ask today is not whether our government is too big or too small, but whether it works – whether it helps families find jobs at a **decent** wage, care they can afford, a retirement that is **dignified**. Where the answer is yes, we **intend** to move forward. Where the answer is no, programs will end.*

And those of us who manage the

joined to common purpose, and when we bravely do what must be done.

Those who doubt fail to understand one key thing: that the ground has moved from under them. And that the old political arguments that have delayed us for so long can no longer be used. The question we ask today is not if our government is too big or too small, but if it works. We ask if it helps families find jobs at an acceptable pay, provides good low-cost health care, and lets citizens retire with respect and comfort. Where the answer is yes, we will move forward. Where the answer is no, programs will end.

And those of us who are in

162

*public's dollars will be held to account - to spend wisely, **reform** bad habits, and do our business in the light of day – because only then can we **restore** the **vital** trust between a people and their government. Nor is the question before us whether the market is a force for good or ill. Its power to **generate** wealth and expand freedom is **unmatched**, but this crisis has **reminded** us that without a **watchful** eye, the market can spin out of control – and that a nation cannot **prosper** long when it **favors** only the **prosperous**.*

charge of the public's money will be held responsible. We must spend wisely, improve bad customs, and do our business in the light of day, because only then can we bring back the required trust between a people and their government. The question before us is not if the market is a force for good or ill. Its power to create wealth and expand freedom is unmatched. But this crisis has demonstrated to us that without an eye to watch it, the market can get out of control. This crisis shows us that a nation cannot gain wealth when it acts only in the interests of the wealthy.

*The success of our economy has always depended not just on the size of our **Gross Domestic Product**, but on the reach of our*

The success of our economy has always depended not just on its size and value, but on the outreach of our national

163

prosperity; on our ability to extend opportunity to every willing heart – not out of **charity***, but because it is the surest* **route** *to our common good. As for our common defense, we reject as false the choice between our safety and our ideals. Our* **Founding** *Fathers, faced with* **perils** *we can scarcely imagine,* **drafted** *a charter to* **assure** *the rule of law and the rights of man, a charter expanded by the blood of* **generations***. Those ideals still light the world, and we will not give them up for* **expedience's** **sake***. And so to all other peoples and governments who are watching today, from the grandest* **capitals** *to the small village where my father was born: know that America is a friend of each nation and every man, woman, and child who seeks a future of peace and*

wealth. It has depended on our ability to give an opportunity for success to every willing heart – not as a handout, but because it is the surest road to the common good. As for our common defense, we reject as false the choice between our safety and our values. Our first fathers were faced with dangers we can hardly imagine, but in that time they wrote a Constitution that established the rule of law and the rights of man. The laws and values of that Constitution were expanded by the blood of our people through history. Those values still light the world, and we will not give them up for the easy way out. And so we say something to all other peoples and governments *dignity, and that we are ready to lead once more. Recall that earlier generations faced down **fascism** and **communism** not just with **missiles** and **tanks**, but with **sturdy alliances** and **enduring convictions**. They understood that our power alone cannot protect us, nor does it entitle us to do as we please.*

who are watching today, from very important cities to the small town where my father was born. We say: You should know that America is a friend to each nation and every man, woman and child who seeks a future of peace and shared respect. You should know that we are ready to lead once more. Remember that earlier people faced down governments of dictators and extreme socialism not just with weapons of war, but with strong ties to allies and lasting beliefs. They understood that our power alone cannot protect us, nor does it give us the right to do as we please.

*Instead, they knew that our power grows through its **prudent** use; our security*

Instead, they know that our power grows through its careful use. They know that *emanates from the justness of our cause, the force of our example, the **tempering** qualities of **humility** and restraint. We are the keepers of this **legacy**. Guided by these **principles** once more, we can meet those new threats that demand even greater effort – even greater cooperation and understanding between nations. We will begin to responsibly leave Iraq to its people, and **forge** a hard-earned peace in Afghanistan. With old friends and former **foes**, we will work **tirelessly** to lessen the nuclear threat, and roll back the **specter** of a warming **planet**.*

*We will not apologize for our way of life, nor will we **waver** in*

our security comes from the justness of our cause, the force of our example, and the calming qualities of respectfulness and restraint. We are the keepers of this tradition. As long as we are guided by these values once more, we can meet those new dangers that demand even greater effort – even greater cooperation and understanding between nations. We will begin to responsibly leave Iraq to its people, and create a hard-earned peace in Afghanistan. With old friends and former enemies, we will never stop working to lessen the danger of nuclear war. We will roll back the warming of the earth that continues to threaten us.

We will not apologize for our way of life, nor will we halt in its defense, and for those who seek to *advance* their aims by *inducing* terror and *slaughtering* innocents, we say to you now that our spirit is stronger and cannot be broken; you cannot *outlast* us, and we will defeat you.

For we know that our *patchwork heritage* is a strength, not a weakness. We are a nation of Christians and Muslims, Jews and Hindus – and non-believers.

We are shaped by every language and culture, drawn from every end of this Earth; and because we have tasted the *bitter swill* of civil war and *segregation*, and *emerged* from that dark *chapter* stronger and more united, we cannot help but

defending it. For those who seek to push forward their aims by bringing about fear and by killing innocents, you should listen. We say to you now that our spirit is stronger and cannot be broken; you cannot last longer than us, and we will defeat you.

For we know that our differing and mixed traditions are a strength, not a weakness. We are a nation of Christians and Muslims, Jews and Hindus - and non-believers.

We are shaped by every language and culture, called forward from every end of this Earth. We cannot help but believe the old hate will pass because we have tasted the terrible drink of civil war and racial injustice. We have *believe that the old hatreds shall someday pass; that the lines of tribe shall soon dissolve; that as the world grows smaller, our common humanity shall reveal itself; and that America must play its role in ushering in a new era of peace.*

To the Muslim world, we seek a new way forward, based on mutual interest and mutual respect. To those leaders around the globe who seek to sow conflict, or blame their society's ills on the West – know that your people will judge you on what you can build, not what you destroy. To those who cling to power through corruption and deceit and the silencing of dissent, know that you are on the wrong side of history; but that we will extend a hand if you are

come out from that dark time stronger and more united. We must believe the lines of race will soon clear away; that as the world grows smaller, our common human nature will come out into the open. And we know that America must play its part in welcoming in a new age of peace.

To the Muslim world, we seek a new way forward, based on shared interest and shared respect. To those leaders around the world who seek to increase anger and bad feelings, or blame their society's ills on the West – your people will watch you. You should know that they will judge you on what you can build, not what you destroy. You hold on to power through breaking of trust and by trickery and by *willing to **unclench** your fist.*

*To the people of poor nations, we **pledge** to work alongside you to make your **farms flourish** and let clean waters flow; to **nourish** starved bodies and feed hungry minds. And to those nations like ours that enjoy relative plenty, we say we can no longer afford **indifference** to suffering outside our borders; nor can we consume the world's resources without regard to effect. For the world has changed, and we must change with it. As we consider the road that **unfolds** before us, we remember with **humble gratitude** those brave Americans who, at this very*

silencing of those who feel and think differently. You should know that you are on the wrong side of history, but that we will extend a hand if you are willing to untighten your fist.

To the people of poor nations, we give you our word of honor. We will work with you to make your businesses grow and to let clean waters flow; we will help feed starved bodies and hungry minds. And to those nations like ours that enjoy comparative plenty, we say this. We can no longer turn a blind eye to suffering outside our borders; nor can we use up the world's resources without thinking. For the world has changed, and we must change with it. As we consider the road that opens

169

*hour, **patrol** far-off deserts and distant mountains. They have something to tell us today, just as the fallen **heroes** who lie in Arlington **whisper** through the ages. We honor them not only because they are guardians of our **liberty**, but because they **embody** the spirit of service; a willingness to find meaning in something greater than themselves. And yet, at this moment – a moment that will define a generation – it is **precisely** this spirit that must **inhabit** us all. For as much as government can do and must do, it is **ultimately** the faith and **determination** of the American people upon which this nation relies.*

before us, we remember with respectful thanks to those brave Americans who, at this very hour, guard far-off deserts and distant mountains. They have something to tell us today, just as the fallen soldiers who lie in Arlington speak softly through the ages. We honor them not only because they guard our freedom, but because they represent the spirit of service; a willingness to find meaning in something greater than themselves. And yet, at this point in time – a day that will define the people of our time – it is this same spirit that must live in us all. For as much as government can do and must do, in the end it is the belief and bravery of the American people on which this nation depends.

*It is the kindness to take in a stranger when the **levees** break, the **selflessness** of workers who would rather cut their hours than see a friend lose their job which sees us through our darkest hours. It is the **firefighter's** courage to storm a **stairway** filled with smoke, but also a parent's willingness to **nurture** a child, that finally decides our **fate**.*

It is the kindness to take in a stranger when the river walls break. It is the workers who think not of themselves but choose to cut their hours so a friend won't have to lose their job. This is what sees us through our darkest hours. It is the firefighter's bravery to storm the steps of a building filled with smoke, but also a parent's willingness to raise a child with love, that finally decides our future.

*Our challenges may be new. The instruments with which we meet them may be new. But those values upon which our success depends – hard work and honesty, courage and fair play, tolerance and **curiosity**, loyalty and **patriotism** – these things are old. These things are true.*

The tests and trials we face may be new. The tools with which we meet them may be new. But those values upon which our success depends – honesty and hard work, strong-heartedness and fair play, acceptance and desire for knowledge, loyalty and

*They have been the quiet force of progress throughout our history. What is demanded then is a return to these truths. What is required of us now is a new **era** of responsibility – a recognition, on the part of every American, that we have duties to ourselves, our nation, and the world, duties that we do not **grudgingly** accept but rather seize **gladly**, firm in the knowledge that there is nothing so satisfying to the spirit, so defining of our character, than giving our all to a difficult task.*

love of country – these things are old. These things are true. They have been the quiet force of progress all through our history. What is demanded then is a return to these truths. What is required of us now is a new age of responsibility – a recognition, on the part of every American, that we have duties to ourselves, our nation, and the world. Those are duties that we do not unwillingly accept but rather take freely and happily. We are strong in the knowledge that there is nothing so satisfying to the spirit, so defining of our nature, than giving our all to a hard job.

*This is the price and the **promise** of citizenship.*

This is the price and the truth of being a citizen.

This is the source of our

This is the beginning of our

*confidence – the knowledge that God calls on us to shape an uncertain **destiny**.*

*This is the meaning of our **liberty** and our **creed** – why men and women and children of every race and every faith can join in celebration across this **magnificent mall**, and why a man whose father less than sixty years ago might not have been served at a local **restaurant** can now stand before you to take a most **sacred oath**.*

*So let us mark this day with remembrance, of who we are and how far we have traveled. In the year of America's birth, in the coldest of months, a small **band** of **patriots huddled** by dying*

trust – the knowledge that God calls on us to shape an uncertain future.

This is the meaning of our freedom and what we hold true – why men and women and children of every race and every belief system can join in celebration across this wonderful public area. And it is why a man whose father less than sixty years ago might not have been served food at a local restaurant, can now stand before you to be sworn in to the most important and respected office of President.

So, today, let us remember who we are and how far we have traveled. In the year of America's birth, in the coldest of months, a small group of nationalists sat together *campfires on the **shores** of an icy river. The capital was **abandoned**. The enemy was **advancing**. The snow was **stained** with blood. At a **moment** when the outcome of our revolution was most in doubt, the father of our nation ordered these words be read to the people: "Let it be told to the future world...that in the depth of winter, when nothing but hope and virtue could survive...that the city and the country, **alarmed** at one common danger, came forth to meet.*

*America. In the face of our common dangers, in this winter of our **hardship**, let us remember these timeless words. With hope and virtue, let us*

around dying camp-fires on the edge of an icy river. The capital was empty – all had left. The enemy was coming forward. The snow was colored with blood. At a time when the outcome of our battle for change was most in doubt, the father of our nation ordered these words be read to the people: "Let it be told to the future world... that in the depth of winter, when nothing but hope and honor could survive... that the city and the country, [awoken to] one common danger, came forward to meet it."

America. In the face of our common dangers, in this winter of our suffering, let us remember these words always. With hope and honor, let us brave once more

174

*brave once more the icy currents, and **endure** what storms may come.*

*Let it be said by our children's children that when we were tested we refused to let this **journey** end, that we did not turn back nor did we falter; and with eyes fixed on the **horizon** and God's **grace** upon us, we carried forth that great gift of freedom and delivered it safely to future **generations**."*

the icy "currents, and make it through what storms may come.

Let it be said by our children's children that when we were tested we refused to let our progress end, that we did not turn back nor did we fall down. And with eyes fixed on the distance and God's goodness to help us, we carried forward that great gift of freedom and delivered it safely to future people."

3 of 137 Pieces in World Press

Robert McCrum - The Guardian

 "The end of Babel is one of mankind's oldest ambitions, and Globish is its most recent expression.... war has given a pacific, neutral voice like Globish a new impetus in the 21st century. This, you might say, is the Globish village."

 **Iman Kurdi - Arab News**

"Globish also teaches us that the more English becomes an international language, the more the ownership of the language will move away from the Anglo-Saxons."

TIMESONLINE **Ben McIntyre - The Times (London)**

"The language they spoke was a highly simplified form of English, without grammar or structure, but perfectly comprehensible, to them and to me. Only now do I realise that they were speaking "Globish", the newest and most widely spoken language in the world.... Globish is not the end of the language, but an important step on the evolutionary ladder, and for many an introduction to the world."

Partial Resources

Council of Europe (2008). *Common European Framework of Reference for Languages: Learning, teaching, assessment*. Retrieved March, 17, 2009, from:
http://www.coe.int/T/DG4/Portfolio/?L=E&M=/main_pag
es/levels.html

Dlugosz, K. (2009) *English Sounds Critical to Global Understanding*. Pécs (Hungary): University of Pécs.

Graddol, D. (2006). *English Next*. London: British Council.

Nerrière, J. P. (2004). *Don't speak English. Parlez globish!* Paris: Eyrolles.

Nerrière, J. P., Bourgon, J., Dufresne, Ph. (2005) *Découvrez le Globish*. Paris: Eyrolles.

Other Sources

Jack Chambers, Toronto University linguist, as quoted in "Parlez vous Globish? Probably, even if you don't know it," Lynda Hurst, *Toronto Star*, March 7, 2009

Notes of appreciation:

- The conversion of President Obama's Inauguration Speech from English to Globish was the idea and the work of Alexandros, a Globish supporter who teaches English in Osaka, Japan.

- Dr. Liddy Nevile, of La Trobe University in Melbourne, and our friend in One Laptop Per Child, contributed moral support – plus extensive editing which made this book a lot better.

Web Sites with Globish Information

www.jpn-globish.com - Original Globish site (much of it in French, but also some in Italian, Spanish and English)

www.globish.com - New Globish portal site

www.bizeng.net (2008 series of business articles written in Globish by David Hon.) **www.bizeng.mobi** (for mobiles)